WOMAN'S HOUR
BOOK OF
HUMOUR

Sally Feldman is joint editor of BBC Radio Four's *Woman's Hour*. Before joining the BBC in 1983 she was editor of *Woman's World* magazine, and previously edited teenage publications.

She has two children and is married to a music journalist and broadcaster.

Also published by BBC Books:
Woman's Hour Book of Short Stories
Woman's Hour Book of Short Stories 2

WOMAN'S HOUR BOOK OF HUMOUR

THE CENTURY'S FUNNIEST FEMALE-WRITING

Selected and introduced by Sally Feldman

BBC BOOKS

Published by BBC Books
a division of BBC Enterprises Limited
Woodlands, 80 Wood Lane
London W12 0TT

First published 1993
Reprinted 1994

ISBN 0 563 36355 X

Set in 11/13pt Garamond by Redwood Typesetting Ltd
Printed and bound in Great Britain by Clays Ltd, St Ives plc
Cover printed by Clays Ltd, St Ives plc

CONTENTS

———————— ◆ ————————

———————————

Contents

INTRODUCTION

◆

*Don't you know the women's movement has no
sense of humour?
No, but play the first few bars and I'll hum along!*

That was the cover of an early edition of *Ms* magazine in
the serious seventies. Nearly twenty years later there are
still those for whom women's humour is a combination as
absurdly improbable as safe sex, military intelligence, lean
cuisine and Superman.

The writer Fidelis Morgan once had a script savagely cut.
'It's got punchlines,' the politically correct director explained
wearily. 'Thanks very much,' replied Fidelis, gratified. 'No,
that's the problem,' the director went on. 'A punchline is a
male construct. Like the male orgasm. Women's humour
must ebb and flow gently like waves.'

Here, you'll find all kinds of satisfaction – from belly
laughs to sardonic chuckles, broad farce to vicious irony.
What these various pleasures have in common is that they are
by women, have been published this century, and have passed
one simple test: they made me laugh out loud.

Among the contributors are novelists and short story
writers, journalists and poets, comediennes and children's
writers. They range from classic humorists – Stella Gibbons,
Joyce Grenfell, Nancy Mitford, Dorothy Parker – to modern
novelists such as Lisa Alther, Muriel Spark, Maureen Freely,
and two romantic writers who have both exploded into
comedy: Sarah Harrison and Philippa Gregory. Established
newspaper columnists like Katharine Whitehorn, Jilly
Cooper, Sue Arnold and Alice Thomas Ellis mingle with
newer ones – Helen Fielding, Libby Purves and Lynne Truss.

I hope you'll relish it, whatever your sex. I don't really

believe there is such a thing as 'women's humour' – except insofar as there are differences between men's and women's experiences. Traditionally these have been quite marked. As one apocryphal wife put it, 'He makes the big decisions: whether to lower the interest rates, how to protect the rain forests, Europe, Russia, things like that. And I make all the little ones: where we live, where the children go to school, what we eat.'

So, as you might expect, there is a good deal of emphasis on things domestic. While a male writer may find humour in men being competent in the kitchen, or will delight in the novelty of a man up against the nappies, women laugh at being hopeless at all the things we're meant to be good at.

'If God is a woman, why is She so short of thunderbolts?' muses Jill Tweedie's faint-hearted feminist. Katharine Whitehorn dedicates her catalogue of *Sluts* to all women who have changed their stockings in a taxi. 'Have definitely failed as Mother, Housewife and Gardener,' reflects Sue Limb's Dulcie Domum. 'Have failed as Drudge too.' Lynne Truss tells us ruefully, 'At my age, women are supposed to hear the loud ticking of a biological clock, but I think I must have bought the wrong battery for mine.'

Americans are less hooked on guilt and apology, more keen on being hard-bitten and cynical. The mother of them all, of course, is Dorothy Parker. Hers is the only book review I've included. It is gloriously bitchy – 'The affair between Margot Asquith and Margot Asquith will live as one of the prettiest love stories in all literature' – yet captures perfectly her acid tongue and soft heart.

Fran Lebowitz, often described as her spiritual descendant, lacks Dorothy Parker's vulnerability – the sadness beneath the wit. But she has inherited all the urban decadence. At 3.40 p.m., she tells us, 'I consider getting out of bed. I reject the notion as being unduly vigorous.' Another latter-day Dorothy is Cynthia Heimel, who laces her sardonic radical chic with something far more lovable. 'If he's the right man, you can have greasy hair, spinach in your teeth and your skirt on inside-out and he'll still be entranced and follow you to the ends of the earth.'

Just as reassuring is Erma Bombeck, a cross between Claire Rayner and Roseanne Barr, who has a novel approach to Weight Watchers: 'We get together every Monday for coffee and doughnuts, and watch each other grow.' Phyllis Diller gets the prize for being furthest ahead of her time – her 'Household Hints', written in 1958, begins with the assumption that you're probably still in bed at 4.30 p.m. and need some emergency advice.

And if it's advice you're after, there's plenty of it. Laurie Graham's *Parents' Survival Guide* does for childcare manuals what Jerome K. Jerome did for river navigation. Suppose you object to your friends' horrible toddler. Easy, she assures you. 'Just take them aside and say "Tim, Patsie, we go back a long way so we know you'll thank us for telling you that Becky is not welcome to sit on her potty during our poker games. We'll call again when she's left home."'

Libby Purves suggests what you should do when the businessman in the hotel room next to yours tries to force his attentions on you. 'Try saying, "Get your hand off my knee, you dirty beast, I've got a Travel Scrabble set here." He'll probably be grateful.'

Maureen Lipman offers a sort of *Karma Sutra* of humour – not just the jokes, but how to tell them. 'All the animals in Jokeland,' she tells us, 'have totally human characteristics.' So, in quick-fire succession, you can meet a competitive dog, a lioness worried about her press coverage, a male chauvinist gorilla and a heroic turkey! Hers are cartoon characters. Other pieces draw on more rounded comic creations like Victoria Wood's Kitty, who has resigned any ambition to lead the country because she's 'been the length and breadth of Downing Street and never spotted a decent wool shop.' In *Heartburn*, Nora Ephron introduces 'the first Jewish Kimberley, so stingy that she made stew out of leftover pancakes.'

Joyce Grenfell has produced a monstrous committee mogul: 'There is one voice among the altos that did not ought to be there.'

Cyra McFadden's chronicle of Marin County Life, *The Serial*, centres round Kate, who'd 'like to take assertiveness training but was afraid Harvey wouldn't let her.' Lisa Alther has fun with the counter-culture, too, with Starshine who is writing *The Lesbian Book of the Dead* and organises the group Masturbation Circle.

What else do women find funny? Well, men of course. Gloria Steinem speculates famously on what would happen if men could menstruate. 'They'd boast about how often and how much.' Men are a favourite topic with poets, too. Fiona Pitt-Kethley writes acidly:

That humans with these fickle bits and bobs
Are given a fairer lot and better jobs.

Wendy Cope has produced the funniest love poem I've ever come across – to a man who drives too fast, makes engine noises, and:

When I ask if this necklace is all right he replies,
'Yes, if no means looking at three others.'

Alice Kahn actually goes over to the other side and becomes a man for the day. 'The first thing I noticed was the frightened look on my husband's face when he woke up and saw me standing there dousing myself with Stud, the after-shave for men who want to make a stink.'

And then there's sex. Women write amusingly about sex because women find sex hilarious. All women do. The straighter-laced the woman, the more hysterical she finds it. Maybe we find it funnier than men do because we have to go through so much more – periods, childbirth, gynaecological examinations, petting. Remember that Joan Rivers line? 'With my first child I can recall screaming, "Get this thing out of me! Get this thing out of me!" And that was the conception!'

So treat this as a storm warning. There are items in this collection you may wish to skip. If you do, you'll miss how Sarah Harrison's heroine finds herself collapsing in a heap with her fanciable dinner-party guest – at the very moment that her son's boy scout troop arrives at the front door; how Germaine Greer lost twenty-four pairs of knickers in one go; and why Florence King has such fond memories of 1955 Chevys – their awkward gear arrangements and their sticky leather seats.

You may well also wish to avoid reading about Dulcie Domum's bad experience with a urine sample and the puzzlement of Miss Jean Brodie's protegées at the whole idea of passionate abandon. 'You would think the urge would have passed by the time she got her clothes off,' they ponder, chewing their toffees frowningly.

The younger you are, the more you expect from the opposite sex – and the more scope there is for disappointment. Richmal Crompton's William reflects, after a bruising first encounter with Violet Elizabeth, that he'll never marry 'some ole girl ... "S'all very well saying *that*," said Douglas again gloomily, "but some ole girl'll probably marry you."' Jan Mark is a children's writer who captures perfectly the teenage state – a mixture of world-weariness and idealism. 'Innocence in adults is terrifying,' one of them remarks laconically. Sue Townsend's Adrian Mole is touchingly in love as only the very young can be. 'Pandora, Pandora, Pandora. Why? Why? Why?'

By the time you get to Helen Lederer's age you have to be more flexible. 'Why shouldn't he see other women friends? I know I do.' Dawn French and Jennifer Saunders do as well, and their friendship is encapsulated in their quirky stage acts. The sketch I've chosen, set in a women's magazine, is brilliantly funny but not to be confused with any well-known radio programmes...

For that, you need to turn to Jenni Murray's account of life behind the scenes at *Woman's Hour* – an affectionate portrait

WILD WOMEN

◆

The closest I've come to being a femme fatale was a serious road accident.
Sandi Toksvig

Women have a much better time than men in this world; there are far more things forbidden to them.
Oscar Wilde

TOO TIRED TO WANT TO GO HOME

Jenni Murray

♦

Thursday night at Woman's Hour's favourite club. The customary wine bottles and crisps mingle with handbags full of scripts and a tangle of tape. Two or three of the producers are flicking idly through a back issue of Hello. Another is putting on her make-up. Someone is giving someone else a massage.

'I must,' Sally slurs, rather more convincingly than is her habit, 'go home.'

'Naw, stay and have another one!' The automatic chorus usually elicits an, 'Oh, go on then, just one.' After all these years the two of us have got it down to a fine art. One more drink means that, with any luck, the kids will already be in bed by the time you roll home. But tonight is different...

'I absolutely must go,' she insists. 'He's leaving at six in the morning. He's flying to the States for two weeks.'

'Working?' I gasp incredulously.

'No, of course not. More research on the book he began twenty years ago.'

'You're going to pack his suitcase?' Is this woman on the turn or what?

'No,' comes the reassuring response. 'He has to show me how the washing machine works before he goes to bed.'

'Have another one anyway.' I pour it hastily, only spilling a

14

bit. 'You'll need it if you've got to run the house and the kids without him.'

'I expect we'll just slide into a slovenly morass,' Sally agrees, watching me rubbing the red wine expertly into the carpet. 'If only we had a cleaning lady.'

'If only we had any money.'

The younger members assume their bored, here-we-go expressions.

'If only we'd married rich men.'

'But what does it matter if he doesn't earn any money, just as long as he loves you.' Arabella, obviously, is a trainee. She is blonde, gorgeous and bright. She is also very young. Sally and I, forty-something, sporting *Cell Block H* haircuts and a continual air of 'I was there in 68,' exchange a world-weary look.

'I have trouble with husbands, too.' Fanny often becomes maudlin as the cheap wine takes effect. 'But it's always other people's. I can't seem to attract anything else. Do you suppose I'm just doomed to be a plaything?'

We all consider Fanny doubtfully. She is dark, pretty, early thirties, vehemently feminist and frighteningly clever. She it was who reduced an entire Radio Review Board to quivering jelly when they dared to question whether three Portuguese women playwrights really merited a ten-part series. She had an announcer in tears for referring to Simone de Beauvoir as Sartre's wife. She pinched Salman Rushdie's bum. The *Guardian* Diary once referred to her as the Amazon full of crocodiles.

'If you're a plaything then I'm a Butlins Redcoat,' I mutter. My attention is caught by Arabella, struggling pathetically with a recalcitrant corkscrew. I try to wrench the bottle from her. She snatches it back. 'Well, if you insist on doing it yourself,' I sniff, 'at least do it right. You must screw and screw until the arms come up.'

'As the Dean of the women's college said to the Bishop,' adds Pat.

Enter Charlie, our token man, eyes and untipped Camel blazing. 'So who laid out two copies of *For Women* on the table in the conference room? Why not just cut them up and let's have male pin-ups all over the office?' Guilt hangs heavy in the atmosphere. Someone stifles a giggle with an 'Uppity Women' hanky. 'Let me remind you,' he pronounces haughtily, 'that a woman who reads *Playboy* is like a Kurd shaking hands with Saddam Hussein. And it seems to me it's time the geese around here started thinking about the sensibilities of the gander.'

'Talking of which,' pipes up sensible Sylvia, producer of that day's programme, 'I don't know what you were thinking of talking dirty to a perfectly nice knitwear designer.'

I look blank.

'You looked straight at that tapestry he was holding,' Sylvia seethes darkly. 'You described the farmyard scene beautifully for the benefit of the listeners. And told him he had a wonderful cock.'

'I wish you'd bear in mind the serial when you make these remarks,' says Pat, amid groans. 'It sounded awful just before *The Turn of the Screw*.'

'Our businesswoman thought it was quite funny,' says Arabella, the peacemaker.

'She can afford to laugh,' I snort. 'All the way to the bank. I just can't get over these women who manage to make a million out of one simple idea.'

'Can you believe it?' Sally agrees. 'All she did was pot up her granny's red cabbage pickle, walk into Harrods and hey presto she's an entrepreneur.'

'So what would we do?' I muse, always one for ingenious ways of making a fast buck, since obviously no one is going to make one for me.

'A parking service for women commuters,' Pat says at once. 'I could let out my driveway in Sidcup for a start.'

'Cake-making for feminists,' suggests Fanny. 'With chocolate contraceptive buttons on the outside.'

'And sponge on the inside.'

'No, even better, what about an all-women plumbing service,' I propose longingly. 'They fix your washing machine at weekends.'

'And provide a man to operate it.'

'What would we call it?' I wonder.

Pat: 'Hot Flushes?'

Sally: 'Little Drips?'

Me: 'The Wet Patch?'

Fanny: 'What a bunch of wimps you are. Why can't you fix your own waterworks?'

Charlie: 'How many feminists does it take to mend a ballcock?'

All: 'One. And it's not funny!'

WOMAN'S WORLD

◆

Dawn French & Jennifer Saunders

Inside the office of the two editors of a women's magazine. There are two desks. There are hundreds of back-issue front covers, with only Princess Di or Jean Boht on the cover. The office is crammed with 'womanly' trivia, catalogues, freebies, Marks and Spencer food, cups and saucers, pretty ruched curtains, chairs covered in Liberty fabrics and a huge pin-board on which there is a layout of the plans for the upcoming edition of the magazine. Fiona (Dawn) is busily pinning up more layouts. She is a well co-ordinated vision in bright silks and large red glasses.

Enter Gill (Jennifer) with lots of carrier bags, huge hand-bag and briefcase. She is a prime example of a mail order victim.

Gill   Morning, I've been thinking about it *all* night, Fiona, and I think I've got it ... Since it's the bumper Easter issue ... bonnets.

Fiona   Bliss ... of course ... bonnets.

Gill   We'll get lots of back issues with pictures of Di in various hats. Isn't it wild and perfect? Now what have we got? Any news from Tim Dalton?

Fiona   Yes, his people have come back. He'll do it so long as he can talk about the new Bond.

Gill	Right, well I think we put him in an Arran and wellies and do 'At home with Bond'.
Fiona	Yes, yes. Not at his home, I hope.
Gill	No, mine, in front of my French windows. Like we did with Anthony Andrews.
Fiona	And we'll call it . . . ?
Gill	Bond, Bond . . . Beautiful Bond? No . . . Terrific Tim? No . . . Tiny Tim? No. Tim Talks?
Fiona	Bond . . . Bond Voyage? No. Premium Bond?
Gill	Perfect, perfect, perfect.
Fiona	I'll get back to Nigel Havers' people and say no.
Gill	Tell them he *could* do a recipe this week, but next week we could do a 'Nigel really is terrific' piece. (*Shouting off.*) Sue, say no to Nigel Havers this week – we're going with Timmy Dalton.
Fiona	I'll write a few letters for postbag this week saying how fab Tim Dalton is and a couple of 'When are we going to see more of Nigel Havers?' . . . or something like that?
Gill	Perfect. Ah yes, now, meant to talk to you about problem page, Fiona, not enough emotion.
Fiona	Well I've written to us with three emotional letters this week.
Gill	Yes?
Fiona	First one is 'Fancy my best friend's husband, what should I do?'
Gill	'Think he feels the same way', that sort of thing?
Fiona	Yes. And the second one is 'Think my best friend's husband has left her but I'm too embarrassed to ask'.

Gill	The answer being a sort of 'She'll tell you in her own time' type of thing?
Fiona	Yes. The third one is 'Not interested in sex anymore – am I abnormal?'
Gill	No, say 'Perfectly normal. If worried, see doctor, he'll give you some pills.' Don't forget to do a 'My daughter's on heavy drugs' item and a letter on Aids: 'Is it all stuff and nonsense?'
Fiona	I'd have to mention sex.
Gill	Oh, then no, drop it, drop it. Now, cover.
Fiona	Well we've got a choice this week, Gilly. Princess Di or Jean Boht.
	Holds up picture of both.
Gill	No competition.
Fiona	Jean Boht?
Gill	Absolutely.
Fiona	We could have her with that pottery chicken from *Bread*, take the top off, and fill it with lots of little Easter chicks inside what do you think?
Gill	'Jean's EASTER JOY!' Marvellous. I don't want to see any primary colours on that cover, only pastels. Gwen, Gwen, something on conservatories. Ask Hannah Gordon or the lovely Susan Hampshire.
Fiona	I thought Shakira Caine on multi-purpose sarongs.
Gill	Good idea.
Fiona	Wait a minute, Gill – sarongs are a *bit* like saris – so we get Shakira on sarongs leading nicely into saris leading nicely into Benazir Bhutto.

Gill   That's our serious piece.

Fiona   We then have the option of putting Benazir's head
           on Margaret Thatcher's body and vice versa and
           that would show our readers what two leading
           women would look like in each other's clothes.

Both   That's our politics.

Gill   Perfect, absolutely perfect. Now, ads? Are we
           carrying tampons this week?

Fiona   (*Very blatant.*) I thought we'd have pantie pads.

Gill   Yes. I mean there's only one place a tampon's
           going.

Fiona   That reminds me, Sue Lawley on flans?

Gill   No. Too spiky.

           Phone rings. Fiona answers.

Fiona   Hello, oh. (*To Gill.*) It's Janey again.

Gill   Asher or Seymour?

Fiona   Asher.

Gill   What does she want?

Fiona   Wants us to cover her kitchen again.

Gill   Oh no. Is there a new angle?

Fiona   (*Into phone.*) Is there a new angle in the kitchen?
           Done this so many times. Yes? Oh, hand-painted
           Mexican tiles.

           They both pull a face.

Gill   No, not Mexican. Say no, but offer her the flan
           feature.

| Fiona | Have to pass on the tiles, bit too ethnic for us – but what about 'It's flantastic' – something about you and flans? Yes? Great. Bye. She's gone for it, novelty flans. |

Gill   Might clash with kids' kitchen.

Fiona   Sue! Can I see the layout for kids' kitchen, pleeeese!

Gill   And Sue! If you're on your feet you couldn't pop down to Marksy's for our lunch, could you? Thank you.

Fiona   Now, Mandy Smith for anything?

Gill   No.

Fiona   Kate Adie?

Gill   What, for a make-over?

Fiona   No. I know she needs a make-over but I've promised it to Sarah's daughter this week.

Gill   Oh well, maybe a travel feature – romantic hot-spots. I know, in Beirut. I've also been thinking Barbara Bush! She's marvellous, isn't she? 'Bumptious, Big, Beautiful, Ballsy Barbara goes grey gracefully ...' something like that? Fiona ...? What's the matter?

Fiona has a sudden turn and is wandering around as if in a dream.

Fiona   It's happening to me again, Gill, I'm sorry. It's suddenly dawned on me that this whole thing is so trivial ...

Gill   Come on, darling, don't be like that ... Come on now ... Pull through ...

Fiona	. . . so pointless . . . it doesn't mean anything . . .
Gill	Come on, sweetie . . . pull through, pull through. We haven't discussed horoscopes yet, come on, pull through, or knitwear . . . come on . . . you can do it . . .
Fiona	Yes, I *do* like horoscopes . . . and there's always the Bride of the Year competition . . . that's important. It's someone's most important day. Isn't it?
Gill	Of course it is, darling. Now, story. What have we got?
Fiona	A thriller by Fay Weldon, seven hundred words, called *He Took Me* . . .
Gill	Too racy! Cut it in half and call it *Regrets* . . .
Fiona	Right.
Gill	So, join me on the sofa for a sum-up meeting . . . We've got Jean's Joy as a cover, and everything I've already mentioned – Di's Easter bonnets, Tim Dalton at home. I know I say it every week, but can't we get Charles Dance to do something?
Fiona	Sue! Charles Dance to do anything.
Gill	(*Reading list.*) Hodge Podge. What's that?
Fiona	Patricia Hodge, back in shape after her baby.
Gill	Lovely. Now, jumpers. Knits are under control, aren't they? (*Shouts.*) Miranda! Now politics.
Fiona	Yes. Bhutto and Babs Bush and Lulu.
Gill	Lovely. Now, science?
Fiona	Well, we've got 'Flossing can be fun'.
Gill	Right, OK. Triumph over tragedy story? I don't see anyone.

Fiona   Sarah Greene.

Gill   Oh yes, all right, that's lovely, and get her to do a salad as well. That will cover environmental issues.

Fiona   Of course, 'Greene's Green Greens'.

Gill   Now, coping with surgery?

Fiona   Yes, Miriam's turned up trumps again. 'Stars and their secret scars.'

Gill   Oh, that's marvellous. Horoscopes, competition, and a free J-cloth offer. That's the bulk of it.

Fiona   We can pad with items from old back issues...

Gill   As per normal. I think that's lunch, Fiona, and a quick afternoon flick through Freeman's.

        She picks up mail order catalogue.

Gill   (*Shouting off.*) Chicken tikka sandwiches, Sue, and a three-bean salad for me.

Fiona   Oh, go crazy, Sue – two syrup sponges.

        Both start flicking through catalogues.

A JOKING ASIDE

◆

Maureen Lipman

You know all those people who say 'Oh, I can never remember jokes'? Like most women for example? Well, I'm not one of them. No, given the right opportunity and a captive audience, by which I mean nailed to the floor, I could happily bore for Europe on the subject of clean ones, rude ones, some as shaggy as your dog. Has this woman no shame?

The first joke I remember was, of course, 'Why did the chicken cross the road?' I didn't get it but I laughed like a drain to show that I did. Later I heard the answer given as 'To see the Duchess lay a foundation stone'. And, this time, I laughed like a sincere drain. '*Lay* a foundation stone, Mam . . . lay . . . oh, forget it . . .' I packed my satchel and chortled all the way to school.

Now I love it when the kids tell me a joke – the more laborious and convoluted the explanation, the better. 'There was this man and this lady. NO, WAIT – I WANT TO TELL IT. And this baby. Er . . . well. Anyway. The plane crashes [*what plane?*] and the baby says "Me not daft" – 'cos the others died, you see – "Me not daft, me not silly, me hold on to Daddy's willy!"' Collapse of stout eight-year-old, clutching stout stomach, and much repeating of punchline in sing-song voice.

Their favourite to date concerns a small squid with a tummy ache lying at the bottom of the ocean. A shark approaches and announces his intention of eating him. 'Please don't!' begs the squid, 'I'm not very well.' 'Come with me,' says the shark, and takes him to the cave of a killer whale. 'Who is it? Whaddya want?' booms the whale. 'S'only me,' says the shark ingratiatingly, 'I brought you the sick squid I owe you.'

All the animals in Jokeland have totally human characteristics. The gorillas talk like Ronnie Barker and the parrots philosophize like E.L. Wisty. No one questions an erudite conversation about sex between a man and his dog on a desert island. As in Disney films, we empathize with their dilemmas despite the indisputable evidence that they have long ears, wet noses and halitosis. Mind you, so do many of the people with whom I hold my most erudite conversations.

Anyway, the dog and the man have been on this desert island for months. They have plenty to eat and drink but their love lives leave a lot to be desired, and they discuss their frustration over many a hot coconut soufflé. One day, while out marmoset-bagging, they chance upon the most gorgeous lady sheep, and both fall passionately in love with her. In order to be fair they toss a coin for who shall court her (that's not how I heard it described, but I have a delicate reader to consider), and the dog wins. Each night after supper, the dog excuses himself and goes off somewhat sheepishly to his lady-love (no doubt singing 'When I'm calling ewe'), and his human friend languishes alone for hours. One day, however, he discovers a beautiful, naked girl washed up by the ocean. She is half dead through exposure and starvation. Gently he wraps her in a blanket, carries her home and slowly and devotedly nurses her back to life. Overwhelmed with gratitude, she gazes at him through sweeping lashes and murmurs, 'Is there anything, *anything*, I can do to thank you for saving my life?' Shyly he demurs, but she persists. 'ANYTHING?' 'Well,' he says, gazing at her longingly, 'well, after dinner tonight ... would you ... would you ... take the dog for a long walk?'

Still on the subject of man's best friend – a scientist was carrying out an experiment to see if animals really took on the characteristics of their masters. The experiment involved putting the dog by an enormous pile of bones to see what he would do with them.

The first was the dog of a mathematician. He studied the bones, separated them into neat piles and finally arranged them into the equation of Pythagoras' theory.

The second dog was the dog of an architect. He piled the bones into a representation of the Pompidou Centre.

The third dog was the dog of an actor. He ate the bones, screwed the other two dogs and asked for the afternoon off.

The most enjoyable jokes are the shortest: 'What's the definition of a Jewish nymphomaniac?' 'Someone who will make love on the same day she's had her hair done.' Boom-boom! What's the definition of Jewish foreplay – three hours of begging. A good Jewish wine? 'Oh you never take me anywhere ...'

I've never had much time for the Shaggy-dog Tale. Too much depends on the phone not ringing during the build-up, and your mother not demanding the potato-peeler during the punchline. Actually, my mother once gave me the perfect intro to a lengthy joke which I'll tell you about. Shortly. It concerned a man having an audience with the Pope in a massive cathedral. He kneels before the altar and a mighty sepulchral voice intones to the tune of the 'Te Deum'. 'What is your na-a-ame?' *Man*: 'John Entwhistle, your Grace, your Holiness, Sir.' *Voice*: 'Where are you fro-o-om?' *Man*: 'London, England, Sir, Your Grace, Lord.' 'What is your business he-e-ere?' 'I dearly wish to convert to Catholicism, your Holiness.' *Voice*: 'What is your occupa-a-tion?' *Man*: 'Please, Sir, I'm a talent scout.' *Voice*: 'Moon River, wider than a mile ...' It's the way you tell it, of course. Particularly after your mother has just said 'Ooh, Maureen, tell them all the joke about "Moon River".'

Have you noticed how jokes always come in batches of

three? Like comic business in a farce? Or bad news? You hear no jokes for weeks, then somebody tells you three. Apparently, the real comedians seldom laugh when they're told a joke. Like doctors, they nod, say 'Ah, ah' and mentally file it away until they can convince themselves they thought of it in the first place. Almost every ethnic minority has a mythology of jokes on its back, and all is fair, I feel, provided that everyone gets lambasted. I once went on *The Parkinson Show*. Michael, I mean. (Mind you, *there's* an idea for an enterprising producer. *The Cecil Parkinson Show*. 'Live from his constituency, he-e-e-ere's Cecil! And tonight's star guest – Victoria Principal!') Sorry, bad taste. Where was I? Michael asked me beforehand to tell my favourite joke. It was, and is, the two Jewish ladies discussing their husbands: *Minnie*: 'Don't talk to me about my Benny. He makes me sick.' *Bella*: 'Why?' *Minnie*: 'Because yesterday he brought me home a dozen long-stemmed red roses.' *Bella*: 'So what's wrong with that? Very nice he should bring you home roses.' *Minnie*: 'You don't know what I have to do when he brings me roses.' *Bella*: 'So tell me.' *Minnie*: 'Well, *first* I have to go into the bedroom! And *then*, I have to take off all my clothes. And *then*, I have to dance around the bedroom. *Then* I have to lie on the bed. *Then* I have to put my legs in the air –' *Bella*: 'You don't have a *vase*?'

As I told the joke the audience gasped. There was a tiny silence of about a week and a half. Then they erupted with a laughter which I thought would never end, and which bubbled up repeatedly throughout the rest of the interview. I had been a fraction worried (a fraction? I bit through the inside of my mouth and was about to bite through Michael's). Most people don't like women telling jokes, particularly risqué ones. Joan Rivers and Marti Caine get away with it by being extremely glamorous and feminine and pretending to be neither. Only Bette Midler really lets it all hang out, and says, 'I am lewd, crude, outrageous and as funny as any man in the joint.' And why not?

Of course, in Liverpool every sentence you hear sounds like a joke. And in Dublin you really understand that Irish jokes are not a form of prejudice, they are everyday language which just happens to be perfectly-scripted dialogue. TV director Bill Hays was in the bath in his Dublin hotel room, when there was a knock at the door. 'Telegram for you, Mr Hays,' said the bellboy. 'I'm in the bath, just push it under the door,' called Bill. 'I can't do that, sor,' said the philosopher on the other side of the door, 'it's on a tray.'

One of my favourite stories concerns an interview for the job of lighthouse-keeper, where the applicants were asked to bring a hobby to counteract the boredom of the job. The Englishman produced Scrabble and a book of crosswords. The Scotsman brought darts and a pack of cards. And the Irishman placed a box of Tampax on the table. The panel expressed amazement and demanded an explanation. 'Well, now, see here,' said Patrick. 'Sure I'd never be bored. For look what it says on here. You can swim, you can go horse-back-riding, you can play tennis . . .'

And now, ladies and gentlemen, at *enormous* expense, the silliest one of all. This one made Christopher Biggins and me fall into a swimming pool, which is a foolproof way of emptying it.

A Martian goes into a pub, and orders a drink for himself and one for everyone in the bar. The publican refuses to serve him, but the Martian just grins affably and repeats his request, adding 'and one for yourself, sir, of course.' Again the publican refuses and again the Martian most reasonably repeats his request (Rule of Three, again, see?). Grudgingly, the publican finally complies, then presents him with a bill for fifty-three pounds. 'Certainly, sir,' beams the Martian, 'I wonder . . . do you have change of a *zoink*?'

Similarly, do you recall the cerebral masterpiece about the two cockney cowboys in the desert – doncha just love the likeliness of all these premises? – and one tells the other he's very hungry.

'Aw, well, partner,' replies the other, 'if you ride a few miles further through the desert, turn right at the cactus mound, you'll find a BACON TREE.'

'Stone me, amigo, 'ave you gone bleedin' mad? There's no such thing as a BACON TREE, yer baccy-chewing twerp.'

'Course there is. I know this desert like the back of me Germans!' (Simultaneous translation: German bands – hands. Cockney rhyming slang/see chiming clang.)

First cowboy rides off into distance. An hour later he returns shot through from stetson to stirrup with arrows.

'That wasn't a BACON TREE, you berk, that was an AM BUSH.'

Mrs Goldblatt in Fortnum and Mason's food department is approached by a liveried floor manager in top hat and tails.

'May I be of assistance, Mrs Goldblatt, Madam?'

'Gimme a qvarter of chopped liver.'

'Certainly, Madam.' He calls out – 'A quarter of a pound of our best French pâté de foie gras for Mrs Goldblatt. Thank you. Will that be all?'

'I vant a half a pound of worst.'

'Certainly, Madam – a half a pound of our finest German salami for Mrs Goldblatt. Will that be all, Madam?'

'No – I vant you should gimme a box lockshen.'

'With pleasure, Madam. A box of our best quality Italian vermicelli for Mrs Goldblatt – and will that be everything, Madam?'

'Dat's all I vant.'

'Thank you. And would Madam like it delivered or will you schlepp it home yourself?'

That one you have to say out loud.

This is no joke – the gardener who had worked for the previous owners of our house was working in the garden one day. He called to me, 'Mrs Rosen – er Mrs Ronel – Mrs er' – my name would forever elude him – 'I've moved that large clump of er – er – whatsits – round to the front bay – the – er – thingummy jobs – you know – the – oh blimey – what are they called? – oh lord, it's on the tip of my tongue – the howsyafathers – doubreys – you know which ones I mean, don't you, Mrs Rosserall – anyway, I've moved them over to the bay – the er – ooo – yes that's it! The forget-me-nots!'

A scriptwriter's dream!

Gorilla jokes are legion. Three elderly Jewish widows, Minnie, Bella and Miriam decide to take a 'vacation with a difference'. Instead of a four-star at Fort Lauderdale, they will go to Africa on safari. All goes well until nightfall when they pitch camp. Without warning, a huge, black, hairy arm comes through the tent flap, picks up Minnie and carries her off through the jungle. Once in a clearing, he throws her on the earth and has his way with her. Once through, he picks her up and charges to the water hole, throws her against the bank and has his way with her. After that, he throws her over his back and thunders through the undergrowth, throws her up against a tree and, would you believe, has his way with her again, ad infinitum and through the nightum.

The next day a search party finds the exposed, exhausted and comatose body of Minnie in a clearing. In a specially chartered ambulance plane they fly her back to the Cedars of Lebanon Hospital where she is placed on an intravenous drip and a life-support machine. Into this scene come Bella and Miriam. To visit. Bella holds Minnie's hand. Miriam weeps. After some minutes, Minnie opens one eye, sees her friends and through parched lips croaks: 'Thoity-three times he had his way viz me. Thoity-three times. In a clearing. On a mud bank. In a tree. In the undergrowth, backwards, forwards every hour all night thru. Thoity-three times. Already. And since then – not a letter – not a postcard – does he call? – Nothing – '

I know it's horribly sexist but, it has to be said, so are gorillas.

Then there's the lonely gorilless whose mate has died just before breeding time, leaving both her and her devoted Irish keeper desolate with grief. The board of directors call a meeting and decide that, to save the zoo the embarrassment of all the advance publicity over a new baby gorilla, they will make Paddy the keeper an offer he can't refuse.

'Paddy, you love that gorilla like a friend.'

'That I do,' replies the keeper.

'Could you see your way for the honour of the zoo, for the future of the Gorilla House and for two hundred and fifty pounds to perhaps making love to that lady gorilla?'

'Can I think it over?' says Paddy.

They agree to reconvene after the weekend.

'Gentlemen,' says Paddy, 'I've decided I'll do it. But only on three conditions. Number 1: no foreplay. Number 2: any children of the union to be brought up Catholic. And Number 3: the two hundred and fifty pounds, could I put down twenty pounds now and pay the rest in instalments?'

Finally, and with ape-ologies to anthropologists and people of delicacy everywhere, I shall tell you of the randy gorilla who, on failing to find local crumpet, sees a lady lioness bending over a water hole and, unable to contain himself, leaps upon her and does his thing. Then, terrified of the consequences, he hurtles panic-stricken through the jungle, pursued hotly by the righteously indignant lioness. Breathless, he comes upon a clearing where a black missionary in a clerical suit is sitting reading *The Times*. The gorilla knocks him out, dons his suit, dog-collar and hat and just grabs the paper in time to be reading nonchalantly when the lioness thuds into sight. 'Have you seen a gorilla running through these parts?' she growls. To which the gorilla replies:

'Do you mean the one who screws lions?'

'Strewth,' cries the lioness seizing *The Times*, 'do you mean it's in the paper already?'

Before I leave the animal kingdom for ever, I must tell you about a man who stopped for petrol in a remote farm in a remote part of New Mexico. The farmer, with his great hospitality, showed him around the farm, where he was amazed and intrigued by the sight of the very friendly turkey who sported a wooden leg. 'What an amazing bird!' he commented. 'Tell me, how did it get its wooden leg?'

'Aw well,' said the farmer, 'that is no ordinary turkey. That turkey saved my life. I was down by the creek one day when I was cornered by a rabid dog snarling and foaming at the mouth. That turkey heard my cry, came running five miles from the barn, leaped for that dog's throat and ripped it apart. Saved my life.'

'That's incredible,' said the traveller, 'but how did it get the wooden leg?'

'And that's not all,' continued the farmer. 'I once got my shirt-tails caught in a threshing machine. Another minute and I'd have been shredded to pieces. Suddenly the turkey stuck its neck round the barn door, saw what was happening, picked up an axe in its beak, hurled it into the engine and jammed the mechanism. Sure saved my life, I can tell you.'

'This is unbelievable!' marvelled the traveller. 'But – how did it get the wooden leg?'

'And that's not all,' the farmer went on, 'I went down to the ocean for a swim one day. Now, unbeknown to me, there was a killer shark lurking round that stretch of water. I was alone when I felt a tug in the current and there on the surface of the water I saw its fin. I was paralysed. Suddenly, from the beach came a strange gobbling sound, and the next thing I saw was the flailing wings of that turkey as it skimmed the water and, with a terrible screech, intercepted that shark's progress. Well, it thumped and it pecked and it scratched and it worried that critter so hard that it turned tail and swam clean off in t'other direction. Damned turkey saved my life again.'

Once more the traveller was overwhelmed with amazement at the turkey's heroism. 'But still,' he insisted 'still – you haven't told me how it got its wooden leg.'

'Well,' retorted the farmer, scratching his beard, 'if you had a turkey that useful you sure in hell wouldn't want to eat it all at once!'

Now, this is verging on the shaggy-dog story and could be,

indeed has been, stretched out for as long as your patience could take it. I generally lose mine unless one is really wonderfully well told. My mother once fooled me totally with a 'true' story about going to see a Paul Daniels show in a Leeds nightclub with a couple of friends. She described how Leslie, the husband, had given Daniels his brand new gold platinum Rolex for one of his tricks, and smiled confidently whilst Daniels smashed it to bits. However, as the show went on and his watch failed to materialize, he got somewhat worried and by the end of the show they were all anxious enough to demand to see the Manager. He seemed terribly nonplussed and took them backstage to meet Daniels' manager. He was profoundly apologetic, thanked them for coming and explained that something had indeed gone wrong with the substitution of the real watch for the fake and as a consequence, Leslie's watch had been smashed. 'Well, you can imagine how we all reacted to that,' said my ma. 'Anyway, his manager was very nice and said, of course it would all be sorted out and the insurance would pay up whatever was needed and intimated possibly more, and would we be so kind as to have tea with Mr Daniels who was very anxious to explain and make further amends.'

She then went on to tell me how very kind and apologetic he was and how they were all served tea and plates of dough-nuts in his dressing-room. All of which she said was most enjoyable.

'Well. [Long pause.] Oh, well, we were all listening to Paul Daniels, when Leslie took a bite of his doughnut – and he suddenly stopped – and you'll never guess what was *inside it* –'

'The watch!' I yelled as though I suspected all along.

'No,' she said, flatly. 'Jam, you silly bugger!'

Ever been thoroughly had? By your own flesh and blood?

Incidentally, before your corsets split – what's the worst thing about Oral Sex? The View.

Don't you ever wonder who it is who's sitting somewhere

under an anglepoise, chewing his pentel, and trying to think up the definitive funny joke? All the time waiting for the phone to ring and Bernard Manning to bark, 'Well, have you done it, I'm on in an hour!'

Whoever he is, I'll bet he's hell to live with. Comedy is, after all, no laughing matter. Aristotle was wont to say, 'Tragedy is an imitation of an action which is serious – with incidents arousing pity or terror – with which to accomplish its purgation of emotions.' Now Ari was a hoot around the Parthenon and a terror with the taramasalata as you all know, but I wonder if he realized that, if you substitute the word comedy for tragedy, exactly the same rules apply.

Every couple of years, some woolly academic gets the bright idea of casting a real 'comic' in Shakespeare. He does this out of desperation with the material in the low comedy scenes. Thus Thora Hird, Dora Bryan, Irene Handl, Max Wall are rediscovered by the press and public. And the implication is always the same – 'My God, these comics can actually ACT!' What's more, they can make inferior, dated tosh zing with freshness and inventiveness. Why not? They've been doing it all their working lives and, quite frankly, after single-handedly saving summer seasons and tv sitcoms, *Pericles, Prince of Tyre* is just a piece of brie.

Knight and dame the lot of them – that's what I say! As we should have honoured Alastair Sim and Margaret Rutherford and Joyce Grenfell and countless others. And while we're at it – let's give our comic writers the same recognition. And while they're alive for a change.

All I'm saying really is when God said 'Let there be light', He meant it. Light doesn't mean insubstantial. No play has ever changed society. But if you change the attitudes of enough individuals, you may eventually improve it. If you leave an Alan Bennett play feeling warm all over and are a mite kinder to your Auntie Edna because of it, then you've got the message. Whether the play had one or not.

By the way. Did I tell you about the elderly Jewish couple

who retired to Brighton? They were sitting on the pier when a flasher in a long mac came running up, opened his mac, exposed himself to Leah. She remained totally impassive. Unable to believe it he returned, re-flashed, and received the same lack of response. The third time he was determined to provoke her. Inches from her nose he whipped open the mac, and stood rigidly before her. After a long pause, she turned to her husband and said, 'You call that a lining?'

Now there's a funny thing...

KITTY

◆

Victoria Wood

Kitty is caught unawares, sipping her fifth cream sherry, and chatting affably to Morag.

No, honestly Morag, I do think that Brillo has helped your freckles. What? Oh, hello. We've been having a running buffet for the last programme. We all mucked in on the nosh; I did my butter-bean whip – it's over there in a bucket. And the director did us a quiche. I suppose it's his acne but I definitely detected a tang of Clearasil.

The producer didn't cook, thank goodness. She's a nice girl, but when someone chain-smokes Capstan Full Strength and wears a coalman's jerkin, you're hardly tempted to sample their dumplings.

Her empty sherry glass is replaced with a full one.

The first day I met her she said, 'I'm a radical feminist lesbian'; I thought, what would the Queen Mum do? So I just smiled and said, 'We shall have fog by tea-time.' She said, 'Are you intimidated by my sexual preferences?' I said, 'No, but I'm not too struck on your donkey-jacket.' Then it was, 'What do you think of Marx?' I said, 'I think their pants have dropped off but you can't fault their broccoli.' She said, 'I'm referring to Karl Marx, who as you know is buried in

Highgate Cemetery.' I said, 'Yes I did know, but were you aware that Cheadle Crematorium holds the ashes of Stanley Kershaw, patentor of the Kershaw double gusset, to my mind a bigger boon than communism.' I said, 'Don't tell me the Russian women are happy, down the mines all day without so much as a choice of support hose?'

Her glass is topped up.

It's all right, leave the bottle. In Russia, show the least athletic aptitude and they've got you dangling off the parallel bars with a leotard full of hormones. And what has China ever given the world? Can you really respect a nation that's never taken to cutlery? We bring them over here and what do they do? They litter the High Street with beansprouts. I know what you're going to say – what about the Chinese acrobats?

Kitty is a little inebriated by this stage.

Over-rated. I could hop up on a uni-cycle and balance a wheelbarrow on my eyebrows but I'm far ... too ... busy. If I was to turn to juggling I should never get any rummy played.

Not that I think Britain's perfect. I see life each week from the train window of my Cheadle Saver, and I think I can safely say, people today aren't pegging enough out.

If I was Prime Minister, and thank goodness I'm not, because I've been the length and breadth of Downing Street and never spotted a decent wool shop. But if I were, I would put a hot drinks machine into the Houses of Parliament and turn it into a leisure centre. The income from that would pay off the National Debt, and meanwhile we could all meet in Madge's extension. I would also put three pence on the price of a flip-top bin, because I don't like them, and use the spare cash to nationalise the lavatory industry, resulting in a standard flush.

I would confer knighthoods on various figures in the entertainment and sporting world, namely David Jacobs, Pat Smythe and Dolly from *Emmerdale Farm*.

Before I leave you, I must say I've much loved coming here every week to put you right, and I'd just like to pass on a piece of advice given to me by a plumbing acquaintance of my father's. It's an old Didsbury saying, and I've never forgotten it.

Kitty has forgotten it. She sits blankly. No, she can't remember it.

COMMITTEE

◆

Joyce Grenfell

The ladies are assembled in Mrs Hailestone's front room somewhere north of Birmingham. The telly is full on. It is time to start the meeting.

Well, let's get down to business, shall we?

Would you be so good as to turn off your telly, please, Mrs Hailestone? Thank you. That's better. It's very good of you to let us use your front room. I think we're all assembled. Mrs Brill, Miss Culch, Mrs Pell, Mrs Hailestone, May and me. All right then, May, let's have the minutes of the last meeting.

Oh, May. You're supposed to have them in that little book I gave you. I told you last time. You're supposed to write down everything we do and say and then read it out at the next meeting, and I sign it.

I know we all know what we said and did, dear, but you have to write it down. That's what minutes are for.

Don't cry, May, dear. Let's get on with the next item on the agenda. Apologies for Absence. You read out the excuses. Oh, May. Well, you must try and remember to bring your glasses next time. All right, I'll read them. Give them here. Cheer up.

Mrs Slope is very sorry she's caught up. Can't come.

Miss Heddle's got her mother again. Can't come.

Lady Widmore sent a telegram: 'ALAS CANNOT BE WITH YOU DEVASTATED'. Can't come.

Well then. As you all know, this is *another* special meeting of the Ladies' Choral to talk about the forthcoming Festival and County Choral Competition. We know the date and we know the set song. Yes we do, May. It's in two parts for ladies' voices in E flat, 'My Bosom is a Nest'.

But of course what we are really here for tonight is this very important question of voices in the choir. Now, we don't want any unpleasantness. Friendly is what we are, and friendly is how we are going to go on. But it's no good beating about the bush, we all know there is *one* voice among the altos that did not ought to be there. And I think we all know to what I am referring.

Now, don't think that I don't like Mrs Codlin, because I do. Yes, she *is* a very nice woman. Look at how nice she is with her little car – giving us all lifts here and there. And she's a lovely lender – lends you her books, and her knitting patterns, recipes, anything. Lovely. Yes, she is a regular churchgoer *and* a most generous donator to the fund. But she just has this one fault: she does not blend.

May, dear, would you be so kind as to slip out and see if I left the lamp turned off on my bike? I don't want to waste the battery, and I can't remember if I did it. Thank you, May.

Ladies, I didn't like to say anything in front of May, but I must remind you that Mrs Codlin's voice is worse than what ever May's was; and you know what happened the last time we let May sing in the competition. We were disqualified. So you see it is very important and very serious.

Oh thank you, May, dear. Had I? I am a big silly, aren't I?

You see, it isn't as if Mrs Codlin had a voice you could ignore. I mean you can't drown her out. They can hear her all down the road, over the sopranos; yes, over your piano, Mrs Pell, over everything. You know, I was stood next to her at practice last week when we did 'The Wild Brown Bee is my Lover'. When we'd finished I said to her very tactfully, thinking she might like to take the hint, I said: 'I wonder who it is stands out so among the altos?' and she said she hadn't noticed. Hadn't noticed! Mrs Brill was on her other side and she said to me afterwards – didn't you, Mrs Brill? – she said the vibrations were so considerable they made her chest hum.

No, I know she doesn't do it on purpose, May.

No, of course she didn't ought to have been let in in the first place. It's ridiculous. It makes a nonsense of music. But the thing is, it was her idea, wasn't it? She founded the choir.

Do you think if anyone was to ask her very nicely not to sing it might stop her? I mean we could let her come and just stand there. Yes, Mrs Hailestone, she does *look* like a singer, I'll give her that. That's the annoying part.

Would anybody like to ask her? Well, has anybody got any suggestions?

No, May, not anonymous letters. They aren't very nice. May...?

I wonder... May, one of your jobs as secretary is watching the handbags and the coats at competitions, isn't it? I mean you have to stay in the cloakroom all during the competitions, don't you? I thought so. Look, May; now don't think we don't appreciate you as secretary – we do, dear, don't we ladies? – But would you like to resign? Just say yes now, and I'll explain it all later. Lovely.

Well, we accept your resignation, and I would like to propose that we appoint Mrs Codlin secretary and handbag watcher for the next competition. Anybody second that? Thank you, Mrs Hailestone. Any against? Then that's passed unanimously. Lovely. Oh, I know it's not an order, Mrs Pell, but we haven't any minutes to prove it. May didn't have a pencil, did you, May?

Well, I think it's a very happy solution. We get rid of her and keep her at one and the same time.

What did you say, May? Can *you* sing if Mrs Codlin doesn't?

Oh, May, you've put us right back to square one.

OUR BODIES, OURSELVES

When I burnt my bra it took the fire department four days to put out the blaze.
Dolly Parton

When a tall, thin, gorgeous blonde walks into a room your first thought is unlikely to be: 'I bet she's got some A-levels.'
Jenny Lecoat

If beauty is truth, why don't women go to the library to get their hair done?
Lily Tomlin

THE FAT BLACK WOMAN GOES SHOPPING

◆

Grace Nicholls

Shopping in London winter
is a real drag for the fat black woman
going from store to store
in search of accommodating clothes
and de weather so cold

Look at the frozen thin mannequins
fixing her with grin
and de pretty face salesgals
exchanging slimming glances
thinking she don't notice

Lord is aggravating

Nothing soft and bright and billowing
to flow like breezy sunlight
when she is walking

The fat black woman curses in Swahili/Yoruba
and nation language under her breathing
all this journeying and journeying

The fat black woman could only conclude
that when it comes to fashion
the choice is lean

Nothing much beyond size 14

GOING WITHOUT

◆

Germaine Greer

Lately I've been thinking that I was getting rather hip where clothes are concerned. I've finally managed to accumulate some that I like, mostly oldies, but most important, they are all comfortable. I don't own a bra or a girdle (or these days a *tight* but that's another story). This complacency was shot from under me by a simple question my brand-new and very respected lady doctor put to me, when preparing to examine me in her 'office' at an elegant address in the East Seventies in New York. 'Why,' she murmured, 'are you wearing pants?'

Now this is no hippy homeopath or herbalist. My doctor wears no charms or beads or sandals, but a good silk dress of Mediterranean length, and greying hair in a simple coil on top of her head. She waited for an answer and I cudgelled my brains for a rational answer, but all that came to mind was a vignette of my mother saying, 'What if you were knocked over by a car?' Obviously, if going without means that one is more cautious in traffic, there's much to be said for it. So I didn't even try saying, 'Well, if I were knocked down by a car ...' 'It's very hot,' she prompted, 'and your skirt is quite ample.' Now once warmth is rejected, as a reason for wearing knickers, what else is there?

I suppose we can give modesty as a reason, provided we accept modesty as a reason for doing anything. But it still won't stand up, because pants themselves are not meant to be seen. If a hurricane were to develop in Bond Street, so that women's skirts were instantly tweaked over their heads, there would be so much other havoc going on that few people would have the leisure to observe whether what was revealed was lingerie or flesh. By the time pants get to be seen, the hour for modesty has passed, be it in the boudoir or the fitting room. (I'm not so sure about the fitting room, but if going without pants means we buy fewer clothes then that is another argument for.)

In any event, knickers are themselves erotic, which might be an argument for retaining them, but not from a woman's point of view, because it is not women who turn on to them. Undie shops run a staple line in playful pantees with clefts in the crotch and cheering inscriptions upon them, all diaphanous and vivid in black and white or red or leopardskin for the truly *farouche*. But apart from the sportive aspect of the knicker, there is also the sinister power of the pant glimpsed at an impressionable age in circumstances of great excitement and guilt, or whatever it is that reduces men to knicker lovers amassing huge piles of them clean or worn, in the corners of rented rooms, begging them from beloved women as an essential prerequisite of sexual satisfaction. If there are no knickers there can be no knicker fixations. Some liberals might think this an impoverishment of the sexual environment – I doubt if the underwear fetishists themselves would agree.

The symbolism of clothes is very muddling. Many women's liberationists have eschewed the skirt for the boiler suit, claiming that skirts mean immobility and availability. Now I know boys who are more intrigued by a front zipper than anything else. A woman in a boiler suit is like a hermit crab: you must wonder and fantasize about her shape. Only reality is an antidote for fantasy. In any case, clothes do not actually influence availability. If all that stands between a male chauvinist and the accomplishment of his desires is a knicker, then you've had it. On the other hand, if you know karate, it doesn't much matter whether you're wearing pants or not. Clothes as protection haven't worked since the knights discovered that their armour hampered them so much that they could be hacked down by the meanest foot-soldier. Ideally, women should not be judged by their clothes any more than men. As long as women are judged easy or provocative because of their chosen mode of dress, they are being judged as beings with significance only through their relation with others. The older generation is often puzzled that women who fling off their clothes at rock concerts are not raped; they do not understand that the connection is not with provocation but with freedom.

One reason I did mumble out to the doctor was, cleanliness, you know, subway seats and all that. But a moment's reflection in the light of her smile revealed that pants are not very hygienic in themselves, or much of a protection against infection, if infection were to be so easily got, which it is not. So, with a great sigh, I put my knickers in my bag and marched off down third Avenue, all unbeknownst to the passers-by breasting a new frontier in a life marked like a tree-trunk by lines of small emancipations.

And yet it was not a new feeling. Long ago in a hotter country, when I was very poor and had few pairs of pants, I was used to going knickerless, but my man would check me up, when he got wise, by running a finger from hip to haunch, feeling for the ridges through my clothes. Then he would march me home, or into a store, so that I could be decently equipped for the day's enterprises. It became a running battle between us, and I guess, if I'd thought it through I'd have realized the significance of the fact that my pants were a good deal more important to him than to me. But we must crawl before we can walk, and later on I accumulated vast stores of pants of all colours, because, unbelievably, I have a tendency to mislay them. I once left twenty-four pairs of pants in a farmhouse in Sicily. I'll never know how the peasants received them.

The troubling thought that remains is that perhaps fewer women wear pantees than I thought. When some friends of mine were working on a construction site underneath a make-shift footbridge in the city, they assured me that one in three women went without. That was in the summer too.

If I had had no pantees I would not have to remember the horrid sight of twelve little stretchy ones all in luminous colours, hanging on the line in a neat row, with all their crotches cut off in a single unbroken line. I was so shaken by the implied threat, that I locked myself in the bedroom until my man came home and we kept the blinds down for ages.

ONE SIZE FITS ALL OF WHAT?

Erma Bombeck

The women in the Mortgage Manor housing development just started a Watch Your Weight group. We get together every Monday for coffee and doughnuts and sit around and watch each other grow. Somehow, it makes us all feel better to know there are other women in the world who cannot cross their legs in hot weather.

The other Monday after I had just confessed to eating half a pillowcase of Halloween candy (I still have a shoebox of chocolate bars in the freezer to go), we got to talking about motivation of diets.

'When my nightgown binds me, I'll go on a diet,' said one.

'Not me,' said another. 'When someone compliments me on my A-line dress and it isn't A-line, I'll know.'

'I have to be going someplace,' said another woman. 'I know as sure as I'm sitting here if someone invited me to the White House I could lose fifteen pounds just like that!' (Snapping her fingers.)

'I am motivated by vacation,' said another one. 'I starve myself before a vacation so a bunch of strangers who have never seen me before can load me up with food so that when I return home I look exactly like I did before I started to diet.'

'Home movies do it for me,' said a woman, reaching for a doughnut.

'You mean when you see yourself and you look fat in them?'

'I mean when they drape me with a sheet and show them on my backside.'

Finally, I spoke up. 'There is only one thing that motivates me to lose weight. That is one word from my husband. My overeating is his fault. If he'd just show annoyance or disgust or say to me, "Shape up or sing as a group," I'd do something about it. I told him the other night. I said, "It's a shame your wife is walking around with fifteen or twenty excess pounds. If things keep going on I won't be able to sit on a wicker chair. What are you going to do about it?" I asked, "Just sit there and offer me another cookie? Laugh at me. Shame me into it! Humiliate me at parties!" Sure, I'd get sore, but I'd get over it and I'd be a far better, thinner person for it. Just one word from him and I'd be motivated!'

'Diet,' he said quietly from behind his paper.

'Fortunately, that wasn't the word. Pass me another doughnut, Maxine.'

A Girl's Inner Security

Helen Fielding

The American writer P.J. O'Rourke once suggested that the ideal pre-marital hen party would involve each guest demonstrating a different contraceptive device to make the others laugh. This summer will see the British launch of a new device, rich in comedy potential, a female condom, to be known as Femidom in this country. (The Swiss, being a famously grown-up and sensible race, have been entrusted with the product this month.)

The notion of a female condom suggests vast swathes of rubber, and prematurely exhausted, absurdly trussed-up women shouting, 'Ready, darling!' in tones of somewhat forced optimism. In fact, the manufacturer, Chartex International, says that in tests involving 1700 couples and 30 000 'usages' in fifteen countries, two-thirds of the participating couples found it 'acceptable'.

I was invited to the offices of a PR company employed by Chartex International for my first viewing. 'Sometimes, when people first see it, they're surprised at the size,' warned the PR lady. (She was fitting me into a busy schedule, promoting, as well as the condom, olive oil, Le Creuset pans and National Prune Week.) Indeed the device does look startlingly hopeful: seven inches long and three times as wide as a normal condom – a clear polyurethane sheath strangely reminiscent of an icing bag, or a rain hat for a small wizard. It is fastened to a bendy ring at the open end, and has another bendy ring loose in the closed end. The loose ring is used to insert the sheath and hold it in place just like a diaphragm. The open end, with the other ring attached, stays outside the body and, during 'usage', as we shall quaintly call it, covers the (WARNING: horrid word coming up) labia.

The condoms will sell at about £1 for three. Each comes in a package similar to the smallest size of chocolate buttons, by no means as discreet as a male condom, but easy to keep in a make-up bag.

Another of the PR ladies had fitted personal Femidom trials into her own busy schedule. She is unable to use the Pill, because of migraine, and other barrier methods, because of allergies, and is unwilling to use a coil. 'As far as I'm concerned it's the answer to my problems,' she says. 'My husband's reaction is that it's a hell of a lot better than a male condom. It doesn't grip itself round the man. It has no odour, it warms to the body temperature. And I had no sense that it was going to fall out.'

But what about the bit left outside the body? 'It didn't affect the pleasure at all,' she insisted. In terms of aesthetics however, there can be little doubt that it is rather unusual-looking. And I couldn't help feeling that there might be some problem with a slight squeaking noise. Anyone whose romantic relationship is inclined to deteriorate into helpless giggling might have a problem.

'It didn't so much squeak, as rustle,' said a friend of mine who tried out the product with her husband. 'He said it's much worse than a male condom. He got bored after a minute and a half because it was so rotten. For me it felt like having a baggy surgical glove inside you. It's a real erotic killer.'

But then, no form of contraception is perfect. The male condom looks pretty funny in position, if you're giddy side out or not used to it. A considerable advantage with Femidom is that, as with the diaphragm, it can be installed before the usage process has actually begun, rather than at the sensitive moment when one is about to be usaged at any second. Plus the Femidom and its masculine guest can be left in place for any amount of tender post-usage calming down, without the risk of accident.

Installation, though, is no trifling matter. As with the diaphragm, a Zen-like state, a sense of being with one's own Femidom, will be necessary. Otherwise you will find yourself with devices and swear-words shooting all over the bathroom, and everyone going off the whole idea.

If the device does catch on, it will undoubtedly alter the sphere of contraceptive etiquette. Male condoms have become more socially acceptable, but some women still feel that carrying them suggests an unbecomingly eager approach, and an unspoken accusation when they are produced. Carrying a device to be worn yourself may prove subtly to be more psychologically comfortable.

On the other hand, the male condom as the one contraceptive device worn by the man, and hitherto the only one giving effective protection against Aids, has brought with it some sense of shared responsibility. The arrival of a feminine device which protects against infection would dump that responsibility firmly back with the woman – perhaps we should all be grateful for the rustling.

In terms of eroticism the Femidom does seem slightly more promising than some related products currently in development – the Unisex Condom garment, for example – a polyurethane bikini with attached sheath, which becomes either a vaginal liner or penis sheath, depending on which sex wears it. There is, too, scope for product improvement along the lines of attractive colours and textures, favoured in the male condom world. Perhaps the worrying protuberant ring could be modified to make it more attractive: a lingerie-style lace effect, say, or some suggestion of rose petals.

Come to think of it, either concept presents a pretty odd imaginative leap. But both would undoubtedly go down a storm at a P.J. O'Rourke-style hen party.

BOSOM BUDDIES AND BADDIES

Sue Arnold

Some timely words of comfort for all those flat-chested women whose dreams of achieving a large, firm, upwardly-mobile bosom, *a la* Jane Fonda, were dashed by last week's report from America about the possible danger of silicone implants. You don't need silicone. A bagful of salt water – sorry, make that two bags-full – does the trick just as effectively and is virtually foolproof.

Even if one should spring a leak (and, short of wearing a cast-iron brassiere, a leak is always a possibility), the result would be no more harmful to the system than being hooked up to a saline drip. A well-known British actress, who had better remain anonymous, had a boob burst while filming in Spain, probably during the jousting session. She took the first plane to Toulouse, got a replacement from M. Henri Arion, the man who invented this method of breast prosthesis, and was back on the set first thing in the morning.

How do I know all this? I got it from the plastic surgeon who pioneered breast implants in this country back in the late Sixties. His name is Phillipe Lebon and he is a former president of the British Association of Cosmetic Surgery. He doesn't do implants any more; facelifts take up most of his practice these days, particularly the popular new mini-lift which you can have done during your lunch-hour and costs £350.

But bearing in mind the disquieting news from the US Food and Drug Administration, it was largely of boobs and especially of large boobs, that we spoke over breakfast, his only free appointment in the week. Having overslept, Mr Lebon was wearing a jaunty deckchair-striped dressing gown over silk pyjamas and looked attractively tousled. I could hear his bath running. He had only just read the report himself and was trying unsuccessfully, because it was still so early (and also because he had lost his address book), to contact international experts on silicone implants to clarify the situation.

If I were considering an MoT on my own decidedly down-at-heel bosom, reduced alas from its former splendour by years of drudgery and child-bearing, Mr Lebon is the fellow to whom I would entrust the delicate mission. His talent for making pneumatic silk purses out of spaniels' ears (the plastic surgeon's term for ageing breasts; to wit, long and droopy with nothing inside) goes without saying. A battery of signed celebrity photographs in his consulting room across the street, left by satisfied customers, says it all.

No, I'd go for Mr Lebon because I reckon he's old enough, rich enough and therefore honest enough only to take on clients he feels he can genuinely improve. The first hurdle is to convince him that you want bigger, better boobs for the right reason. To make your errant husband fall in love with you all over again with your new 44 double D cup is not a good reason. Mr Lebon has shown many a pair of spaniels' ears the door because they were only doing it to get something or to please someone. 'You've got to want it for yourself,' he said.

Before getting to grips with the methods of breast augmentation, we straightened ourselves out a bit. We turned off the bath, reheated the coffee in the microwave and discussed the pros and cons of turning the spare lavatory into a Russian vapour cabinet. Mr Lebon said he always liked to put people at ease – it has become an instinct with him. Sometimes without realising it, he drops into a client's regional accent;

thus a Yorkshire matron might be asked to 'strip off t'top and show uz tha tits, luv'.

How much did I know, he wondered, moving a pile of newspapers (we were still hunting for his address book) about the structure of the breast? Not a lot, I admitted. 'Well, we'd better begin with a demonstration', and led me into the dining-room, where we searched among parking tickets, books, apples and photographs for what I imagined to be an anatomical model. 'I was looking for the grapes but I must have eaten them last night,' he said at length. 'Pity, a bunch of grapes is a perfect replica of the workings of the mammary gland.'

Back in the Dark Ages of breast implants, the surgeon would simply lop a chunk off his patient's buttocks, fold it in half, skin and all, and stuff it into the patient's drooping dugs. This was fine at first, but sometimes the implant would ossify, turning innocent love-play into lethal unarmed combat. Then came the first artificial implant. Mr Lebon used something called etheron, which looked and felt like that wool you use to clean saucepans. And then came the amazing arion water-bag – its beauty, from a surgical point of view, being its simplicity.

A tiny incision under the arm, a judicious jiggle with the surgeon's forefinger to make space for the bag, top up with water depending on the size required, seal tightly – and *voilà*. Aesthetically, they look and feel far more realistic than silicone because they move. Remember what Richard Burton said to Liz Taylor after she'd had hers done. 'Bobble your baubles over here, darling', he'd say. Silicone doesn't bobble. ... When I got home, the children were making water bombs by filling balloons and chucking them at each other until they burst. It looked horribly painful. On second thoughts, I'll skip that MoT.

Besides, some people find spaniels and their ears charming.

AEROBICS

◆

Pam Ayres

Well Mother, did I make a fool of myself,
    Last night on the bathroom floor,
I'm so out of shape so I put on the tape
That I sent to the TV for,
Well on came the voice of the expert,
With advice to be careful and slow,
But I thought I knew best, I flung off me vest,
And I thought 'Right-O Mother, let's go!'

I bought my John McEnroe trainers,
My how expensive they've grown
But the thing with this pair, is if I'm not there,
They can run round the block on their own.
I did buy my husband some Reeboks,
I'm afraid they're too high-tech for me,
You pump up the slack, flames shoot out the back,
And you slow down this side of Dundee.

Then I did bicycling exercises,
By Golly, I gave it what for,
Flat on me back with me knees going 'crack'
As the draught whistled under the door,
I borrowed your leotard Mother,
The one that enhances me charms,
Thanks very much but it went at the crutch
When I started rotating me arms.

I bought my dear husband a tracksuit,
He said terry towelling is best,
With a curl of his lip, he did up the zip,
And took all the hair off his chest,
And I bought him an exercise cycle,
The price would have made a man wince,
He never got *off* for a fortnight,
And he's never been *on* the thing since!

We thought we might go on a fun run,
We went with a very nice friend,
He'd not run before and he won't any more,
No, they stretchered him off in the end.
I have had a dabble at tennis,
I jog now and then and I swim,
And I've just met this yoga instructor ...
I'm off for a dabble with him!

TRUE
ROMANCES

◆

Why is it no one ever sent me yet
One perfect limousine, do you suppose?
Ah no, it's always just my luck to get
One perfect rose.
Dorothy Parker

THE SWEET LITTLE
GIRL IN WHITE

◆

Richmal Crompton

The Hall stood empty most of the year, but occasionally tenants re-awoke the passing interest of the village in it. This summer it was taken by a Mr and Mrs Bott with their daughter. Mr Bott's name decorated most of the hoardings of his native country. On these hoardings citizens of England were urged to safeguard their digestion by taking Bott's Sauce with their meat. After reading Bott's advertisements one felt convinced that any food without Bott's Sauce was rank poison. One even felt that it would be safer to live on Bott's Sauce alone. On such feelings had Mr Bott – as rubicund and rotund as one of his own bottles of sauce – reared a fortune sufficient to enable him to take the Hall for the summer without, as the saying is, turning a hair.

William happened to be sitting on the fence by the side of the road when the motor containing Mr and Mrs Bott – both stout and overdressed – and Miss Violet Elizabeth Bott and Miss Violet Elizabeth Bott's nurse flashed by. William was not interested. He was at the moment engaged in whittling a stick and watching the antics of his mongrel, Jumble, as he caught and worried each shaving. But he had a glimpse of a small child with an elaborately curled head and an elaborately flounced white dress sitting by an elaborately uniformed nurse. He gazed after the equipage scowling.

'Huh!' he said, and it is impossible to convey in print the scorn of that monosyllable as uttered by William, '*a girl!*'

Then he returned to his whittling.

William's mother met Mrs Bott at the vicar's. Mrs Bott, who always found strangers more sympathetic than people who knew her well, confided her troubles to Mrs Brown. Her troubles included her own rheumatism, Mr Bott's liver, and the carelessness of Violet Elizabeth's nurse.

'Always reading these here novelettes, the girl is. I hope you'll come and see me, dear, and didn't someone say you had a little boy? Do bring him. I want Violet Elizabeth to get to know some nice little children.'

Mrs Brown hesitated. She was aware that none of her acquaintances would have described William as a nice little child. Mrs Bott misunderstood her hesitation. She laid a fat ringed hand on her knee.

'I know, dear. You're careful who the little laddie knows, like me. Well now, you needn't worry. I've brought up our Violet Elizabeth most particular. She's a girlie who wouldn't do your little boysie any harm . . .'

'Oh,' gasped Mrs Brown, 'it's not that.'

'Then you'll come, dearie, and bring the little boysie with you, won't you?'

She took Mrs Brown's speechlessness for consent.

'*Me?*' said William indignantly. 'Me go to tea with that ole girl? *Me?*'

'She – she's a nice little girl,' said Mrs Brown weakly.

'I saw her,' said William scathingly, 'curls and things.'

'Well, you must come. She's expecting you.'

'I only hope,' said William sternly, 'that she won't 'spect me to *talk* to her.'

'She'll expect you to *play* with her, I'm sure,' said his mother.

'Play!' said William. '*Play?* With a girl? *Me?* Huh!'

William, pale and proud, and dressed in his best suit, his

heart steeled to his humiliating fate, went with his mother to the Hall the next week. He was silent all the way there. His thoughts were too deep for words. Mrs Brown watched him anxiously.

An over-dressed Mrs Bott was sitting in an over-furnished drawing-room. She rose at once with an over-effusive smile and held out over-ringed hands.

'So you've brought dear little boysie,' she began.

The over-effusive smile died away before the look that William turned on her.

'Er – I hadn't thought of him quite like that,' she said weakly, 'but I'm sure he's sweet,' she added hastily.

William greeted her coldly and politely, then took his seat and sat like a small statue scowling in front of him. His hair had been brushed back with so much vigour and application of liquid that it looked as if it were painted on his head.

'Would you like to look at a picture book, boysie?' she said.

William did not answer. He merely looked at her and she hastily turned away to talk to Mrs Brown. She talked about her rheumatism and Mr Bott's liver and the incompetence of Violet Elizabeth's nurse.

Then Violet Elizabeth entered. Violet Elizabeth's fair hair was not naturally curly but as the result of great daily labour on the part of the much-maligned nurse it stood up in a halo of curls round her small head. The curls looked almost, if not quite, natural. Violet Elizabeth's small pink and white face shone with cleanliness. Violet Elizabeth was so treasured and guarded and surrounded with every care that her small pink and white face had never been known to do anything else except shine with cleanliness. But the *pièce de résistance* about Violet Elizabeth's appearance was her skirts. Violet Elizabeth was dressed in a white lace-trimmed dress with a blue waistband and beneath the miniature blue waistband, her skirts stood out like a tiny ballet dancer's in a filmy froth of lace-trimmed petticoats. From this cascade emerged Violet

Elizabeth's bare legs, to disappear ultimately into white silk socks and white buckskin shoes.

William gazed at this engaging apparition in horror.

'Good afternoon,' said Violet Elizabeth primly.

'Good afternoon,' said William in a hollow voice.

'Take the little boysie into the garden, Violet Elizabeth,' said her mother, 'and play with him nicely.'

William and Violet Elizabeth eyed each other apprehensively.

'Come along, boy,' said Violet Elizabeth at last, holding out a hand.

William ignored the hand and with the air of a hero bound to his execution, accompanied Violet Elizabeth into the garden.

Mrs. Brown's eyes followed them anxiously.

'Whath your name?' said Violet Elizabeth.

She lisped! She would, thought William bitterly, with those curls and those skirts. She would. He felt at any rate relieved that none of his friends could see him in the unmanly situation – talking to a kid like that – all eyes and curls and skirts.

'William Brown,' he said, distantly, looking over her head as if he did not see her.

'How old are you?'

'Eleven.'

'My nameth Violet Elizabeth.'

He received the information in silence.

'I'm thix.'

He made no comment. He examined the distant view with an abstracted frown.

'Now you muth play with me.'

William allowed his cold glance to rest upon her.

'I don't play little girls' games,' he said scathingly. But Violet Elizabeth did not appear to be scathed.

'Don' you know any little girlth?' she said pityingly. 'I'll teach you little girlth gameth,' she added pleasantly.

'I don't *want* to,' said William. 'I don't *like* them. I don't *like* little girls' games. I don't want to know 'em.'

Violet Elizabeth gazed at him open-mouthed.

'Don't you *like* little girlth?' she said.

'*Me?*' said William with superior dignity. 'Me? I don't know anything about 'em. Don't want to.'

'D-don't you like me?' quavered Violet Elizabeth in incredulous amazement. William looked at her. Her blue eyes filled slowly with tears, her lips quivered.

'I like you,' she said. 'Don't you like me?'

William stared at her in horror.

'You – you *do* like me, don't you?'

William was silent.

A large shining tear welled over and trickled down the small pink cheek.

'You're making me cry,' sobbed Violet Elizabeth. 'You are. You're making me cry, 'cause you won't say you like me.'

'I – I do like you,' said William desperately. 'Honest – I do. Don't cry. I do like you. Honest!'

A smile broke through the tear-stained face.

'I'm tho glad,' she said simply. 'You like all little girlth, don't you?' She smiled at him hopefully. 'You, do don't you?'

William, pirate and Red Indian and desperado, William, woman-hater and girl-despiser, looked round wildly for escape and found none.

Violet Elizabeth's eyes filled with tears again.

'You *do* like all little girlth, don't you?' she persisted with quavering lip. 'You do, don't you?'

It was a nightmare to William. They were standing in full view of the drawing-room window. At any moment a grown-up might appear. He would be accused of brutality, of making little Violet Elizabeth cry. And, strangely enough, the sight of Violet Elizabeth with tear-filled eyes and trembling lips made him feel that he must have been brutal indeed. Beneath his horror he felt bewildered.

'Yes, I do,' he said hastily, 'I do. Honest I do.'

She smiled again radiantly through her tears. 'You with you wath a little girl, don't you?'

'Er – yes. Honest I do,' said the unhappy William.

'Kith me,' she said raising her glowing face.

William was broken.

He brushed her cheek with his.

'Thath not a kith,' said Violet Elizabeth.

'It's my kind of a kiss,' said William.

'All right. Now leth play fairieth. I'll thow you how.'

On the way home Mrs Brown, who always hoped vaguely that little girls would have a civilising effect on William, asked William if he had enjoyed it. William had spent most of the afternoon in the character of a gnome attending upon Violet Elizabeth in the character of the fairy queen. Any attempt at rebellion had been met with tear-filled eyes and trembling lips. He was feeling embittered with life.

'If all girls are like that . . .' said William, 'well, when you think of all the hundreds of girls there must be in the world – well, it makes you feel sick.'

Never had liberty and the comradeship of his own sex seemed sweeter to William than it did the next day when he set off whistling carelessly, his hands in his pockets, Jumble at his heels, to meet Ginger and Douglas across the fields.

'You didn't come yesterday,' they said when they met. They had missed William, the leader.

'No,' he said shortly, 'went out to tea.'

'Where?' they said with interest.

'Nowhere in particular,' said William inaccurately. A feeling of horror overcame him at the memory. If they knew – if they'd seen . . . He blushed with shame at the very thought. To regain his self-respect he punched Ginger and knocked off Douglas's cap. After the slight scuffle that ensued they set off down the road.

'What'll we do this morning?' said Ginger.

It was sunny. It was holiday time. They had each other and

a dog. Boyhood could not wish for more. The whole world lay before them.

'Let's go trespassin',' said William the lawless.

'Where?' enquired Douglas.

'Hall woods – and take Jumble.'

'That ole keeper said he'd tell our fathers if he caught us in again,' said Ginger.

'Lettim!' said William, with a dare-devil air, slashing at the hedge with a stick. He was gradually recovering his self-respect. The nightmare memories of yesterday were growing faint. He flung a stone for the eager Jumble and uttered his shrill unharmonious war whoop. They entered the woods, William leading. He swaggered along the path. He was William, desperado, and scorner of girls. Yesterday was a dream. It must have been. No mere girl would dare even to speak to him. He had never played at fairies with a girl – he, William the pirate king, the robber chief.

'William!'

He turned, his proud smile frozen in horror.

A small figure was flying along the path behind them – a bare-headed figure with elaborate curls and very short lacy bunchy skirts and bare legs with white shoes and socks.

'William, *darling!* I thaw you from the nurthery window coming along the road and I ethcaped. Nurth wath reading a book and I ethcaped. Oh, William darling, play with me again, *do*. It *wath* so nith yethterday.'

William glared at her speechless. He was glad of the presence of his manly friends, yet horrified as to what revelations this terrible young female might make, disgracing him for ever in their eyes.

'Go away,' he said sternly at last, 'we aren't playing girls' games.'

'We don't like girls,' said Ginger contemptuously.

'William doth,' she said indignantly. 'He thaid he did. He thaid he liked all little girlth. He thaid he withed he wath a little girl. He kithed me an' played fairieth with me.'

A glorious blush of rich and dark red overspread William's countenance.

'*Oh!*' he ejaculated as if astounded at the depth of her untruthfulness, but it was not convincing.

'Oh, you *did!*' said Violet Elizabeth. Somehow that was convincing. Ginger and Douglas looked at William rather coldly. Even Jumble seemed to look slightly ashamed of him.

'Well, come along,' said Ginger, 'we can't stop here all day talking – to a *girl*.'

'But I want to come with you,' said Violet Elizabeth. 'I want to play with you.'

'We're going to play boys' games. You wouldn't like it,' said Douglas who was somewhat of a diplomatist.

'I *like* boyth gameth,' pleaded Violet Elizabeth, and her blue eyes filled with tears, '*pleath* let me come.'

'All right,' said William. 'We can't stop you comin'. Don't take any notice of her,' he said to the others. 'She'll soon get tired of it.'

They set off. William, for the moment abashed and deflated, followed humbly in their wake.

In a low-lying part of the wood was a bog. The bog was always there but as it had rained in the night the bog today was particularly boggy. It was quite possible to skirt this bog by walking round it on the higher ground, but William and his friends never did this. They preferred to pretend that the bog surrounded them on all sides as far as human eye could see and that at one false step they might sink deep in the morass never to be seen again.

'Come along,' called William who had recovered his spirits and position of leadership. 'Come along, my brave fellows . . . tread careful or instant death will be your fate, and don't take any notice of her, she'll soon have had enough.'

For Violet Elizabeth was trotting gaily behind the gallant band.

They did not turn round or look at her, but they could not help seeing her out of the corners of their eyes. She plunged into the bog with a squeal of delight and stamped her elegant white-clad feet into the black mud.

'Ithn't it lovely?' she squealed. 'Dothn't it feel nith – all thquithy between your toth – ithn't it *lovely*? I *like* boyth gameth.'

They could not help looking at her when they emerged. As fairy-like as ever above, her feet were covered with black mud up to above her socks. Shoes and socks were sodden.

'Ith a *lovely* feeling!' she commented delightedly on the other side. 'Leth do it again.'

But William and his band remembered their manly dignity and strode on without answering. She followed with short dancing steps. Each of them carried a stick with which they smote the air or any shrub they passed. Violet Elizabeth secured a stick and faithfully imitated them. They came to a clear space in the wood, occupied chiefly by giant blackberry bushes laden with fat ripe berries.

'Now, my brave fellows,' said William, 'take your fill. 'Tis well we have found this bit of food or we would e'en have starved, an' don' help her or get any for her an' let her get all scratched an' she'll socn have had enough.'

They fell upon the bushes. Violet Elizabeth also fell upon the bushes. She crammed handfuls of ripe blackberries into her mouth. Gradually her pink and white face became obscured beneath a thick covering of blackberry juice stain. Her hands were dark red. Her white dress had lost its whiteness. It was stained and torn. Her bunchy skirts had lost their bunchiness. The brambles tore at her curled hair and drew it into that state of straightness for which Nature had meant it. The brambles scratched her face and arms and legs. And still she ate.

'I'm getting more than any of you,' she cried. 'I geth I'm getting more than any of you. And I'm getting all of a *meth*. Ithn't it *fun*? I like boyth gameth.'

They gazed at her with a certain horrified respect and apprehension. Would they be held responsible for the strange change in her appearance?

They left the blackberry bushes and set off again through the wood. At a sign from William they dropped on all fours and crept cautiously and (as they imagined) silently along the path. Violet Elizabeth dropped also upon her scratched and blackberry stained knees.

'Look at me,' she shrilled proudly. 'I'm doing it too. Juth like boyth.'

'Sh!' William said fiercely.

Violet Elizabeth 'sh'd' obediently and for a time crawled along contentedly.

'Are we playin' bein' animalth?' she piped at last.

'Shut *up!*' hissed William.

Violet Elizabeth shut up – except to whisper to Ginger who was just in front, 'I'm a thnail – what you?' Ginger did not deign to reply.

At a sign from their leader that all danger was over the Outlaws stood upright. William had stopped.

'We've thrown 'em off the scent,' he said scowling, 'but danger s'rounds us on every side. We'd better plunge into the jungle an' I bet she'll soon've had enough of plungin' into the jungle.'

They left the path and 'plunged' into the dense, shoulder-high undergrowth. At the end of the line 'plunged' Violet Elizabeth. She fought her way determinedly through the bushes. She left remnants of her filmy skirts on nearly every bush. Long spidery arms of brambles caught at her hair again and pulled out her curls. But Violet Elizabeth liked it. 'Ithn't it *fun?*' she piped as she followed.

Under a large tree William stopped.

'Now we'll be Red Indians,' he said, 'an' go huntin'. I'll be Brave Heart same as usual and Ginger be Hawk Face and Douglas be Lightning Eye.'

'An' what shall I be?' said the torn and stained and wild-headed apparition that had been Violet Elizabeth.

Douglas took the matter in hand.

'What thall I be?' he mimicked shrilly, 'what thall I be? What thall I be?'

Violet Elizabeth did not run home in tears as he had hoped she would. She laughed gleefully.

'It doth thound funny when you thay it like that!' she said delightedly. 'Oh, it doth! Thay it again! Pleeth thay it again.'

Douglas was nonplussed.

'Anyway,' he said, 'you jolly well aren't going to play, so there.'

'*Pleath* let me play,' said Violet Elizabeth. 'Pleath.'

'*No*. Go away!'

William and Ginger secretly admired the firm handling of this female by Douglas.

'*Pleath*, Douglath.'

'*No!*'

Violet Elizabeth's blue eyes, fixed pleadingly upon him, filled with tears. Violet Elizabeth's underlip trembled.

'You're making me cry,' she said. A tear traced its course down the blackberry stained cheek.

'*Pleath*, Douglath.'

Douglas hesitated and was lost. 'Oh, well – ' he said.

'Oh, thank you, dear Douglath,' said Violet Elizabeth. 'What thall I be?'

'Well,' said William to Douglas sternly. 'Now you've *let* her play I s'pose she'd better be a squaw.'

'A thquaw,' said Violet Elizabeth joyfully, 'what thort of noith doth it make?'

'It's a Indian lady and it doesn't make any sort of a noise,' said Ginger crushingly. 'Now we're going out hunting and you stay and cook the dinner.'

'All right,' said Violet Elizabeth obligingly. 'Kith me good-bye.'

Ginger stared at her in horror.

'But you mutht,' she said, 'if you're going out to work an' I'm going to cook the dinner, you mutht kith me good-bye. They do.'

'I don't,' said Ginger.

She held up her small face.

'*Pleath*, Ginger.'

Blushing to his ears Ginger just brushed her cheek with his. William gave a derisive snort. His self-respect had returned. Douglas's manly severity had been overborne. Ginger had been prevailed upon to kiss her. Well, they couldn't laugh at him now. They jolly *well* couldn't. Both were avoiding his eye.

'Well, go off to work, dear William and Douglas and Ginger,' said Violet Elizabeth happily, 'an I'll cook.'

Gladly the hunters set off.

The Red Indian game had palled. It had been a success while it lasted. Ginger had brought some matches and over her purple layer of blackberry juice the faithful squaw now wore a layer of black from the very smoky fire they had at last managed to make.

'Come on,' said William, 'let's set out looking for adventures.'

They set off single file as before, Violet Elizabeth bringing up the rear, Jumble darting about in ecstatic searches for imaginary rabbits. Another small bog glimmered ahead. Violet Elizabeth, drunk with her success as a squaw, gave a scream.

'Another thquithy plath,' she cried. 'I want to be firtht.'

She flitted ahead of them, ran to the bog, slipped and fell into it face forward.

She arose at once. She was covered in black mud from head to foot. Her face was a black mud mask. Through it her teeth flashed in a smile. 'I juth thlipped,' she explained.

A man's voice came suddenly from the main path through the wood at their right.

'Look at 'em – the young rascals! Look at 'em! An' a dawg! Blarst 'em! Er-r-r-r-r!'

The last was a sound expressive of rage and threatening.

'Keepers!' said William. 'Run for your lives, braves. Come on, Jumble.'

They fled through the thicket.

'Pleath,' gasped Violet Elizabeth in the rear, 'I can't run as fatht ath that.'

It was Ginger and Douglas who came back to hold her hands. For all that they ran fleetly, dashing through the undergrowth where the keepers found it difficult to follow, and dodging round trees. At last, breathlessly, they reached a clearing and in the middle of it a cottage as small and attractive as a fairy tale cottage. The door was open. It had an empty look. They could hear the keepers coming through the undergrowth shouting.

'Come in here,' gasped William. 'It's empty. Come in and hide till they've gone.'

The four ran into a spotlessly clean little kitchen, and Ginger closed the door. The cottage was certainly empty. There was not a sound.

'Ithn't it a thweet little houth?' panted Violet Elizabeth.

'Come upstairs,' said Douglas. 'They might look in here.'

The four, Jumble scrambling after them, clattered up the steep narrow wooden stairs and into a small and very clean bedroom.

'Look out of the window and see when they go past,' commanded William, 'then we'll slip out and go back.'

Douglas peeped cautiously out of the window. He gave a gasp.

'They – they're not goin' past,' he said, 'They – they're comin' in at the door.'

The men's voices could be heard below.

'Comin' in here – the young rascals! Look at their footmarks, see? What'll my old woman say when she gets home?'

'They've gone upstairs, too. Look at the marks. Blarst 'em!'

William went to the window, holding Jumble beneath his arm.

'We can easily climb down by this pipe,' he said quickly. 'Then we'll run back.'

He swung a leg over the window sill, prepared to descend with Jumble clinging round his neck, as Jumble was trained to do. Jumble's life consisted chiefly of an endless succession of shocks to the nerves.

Ginger and Douglas prepared to follow.

The men's footsteps were heard coming upstairs when a small voice said plaintively, 'Pleath – pleath, I can't do that. Pleath, you're not going to leave me, are you?'

William put back his foot.

'We – we can't leave her,' he said. Ginger and Douglas did not question their leader's decision. They stood in a row facing the door while the footsteps drew nearer.

The door burst open and the two keepers appeared.

'Now, yer young rascals – we've got yer!'

Into Mr Bott's library were ushered two keepers, each leading two children by the neck. One held two rough-looking boys. The other held a rough-looking boy and a rough-looking little girl. A dejected-looking mongrel followed the procession.

'Trespassin', sir,' said the first keeper, 'trespassin' an' a-damagin' of the woods. Old 'ands, too. Seen 'em at it before but never caught 'em till now. An' a *dawg* too. It's an example making of they want, sir. They want prosecutin' if I may make so bold. A-damagin' of the woods and a-bringing of a dawg – '

Mr Bott who was new to squiredom and had little knowledge of what was expected of him and moreover was afflicted at the moment with severe private domestic worries, cast a harassed glance at the four children. His glance rested upon Violet Elizabeth without the faintest flicker of recognition.

He did not recognise her. He knew Violet Elizabeth. He saw her at least once or almost once a day. He knew her quite well. He knew her by her ordered flaxen curls, pink and white face and immaculate bunchy skirts. He did not know this little creature with the torn, stained, bedraggled dress (there was nothing bunchy about it now) whose extreme dirty face could just be seen beneath the tangle of untidy hair that fell over her eyes. She watched him silently and cautiously. Just as he was going to speak Violet Elizabeth's nurse entered. It says much for Violet Elizabeth's disguise that her nurse only threw her a passing glance. Violet Elizabeth's nurse's eyes were red-rimmed.

'Please, sir, Mrs Bott says is there any news?'

'No,' said Mr Bott desperately. 'Tell her I've rung up the police every minute since she sent last. How is she?'

'Please, sir, she's in hysterics again.'

Mr Bott groaned.

Ever since Violet Elizabeth's disappearance Mrs Bott had been indulging in hysterics in her bedroom and taking it out of Violet Elizabeth's nurse. In return Violet Elizabeth's nurse had hysterics in the nursery and took it out of the nursery maid. In return the nursery maid had hysterics in the kitchen and took it out of the kitchen maid. The kitchen maid had no time for hysterics but she took it out of the cat.

'Please, sir, she says she's too ill to speak now. She told me to tell you so, sir.'

Mr Bott groaned again. Suddenly he turned to the four children and their keepers.

'You've got their names and addresses, haven't you? Well, see here, children. Go out and see if you can find my little gal for me. She's lost. Look in the woods and round the village and – everywhere. And if you find her I'll let you off. See?'

They murmured perfunctory thanks and retired, followed by Violet Elizabeth who had not uttered one word within her paternal mansion.

In the woods they turned on her sternly.

'It's you he wants. You're her.'

'Yeth,' agreed the tousled ragamuffin who was Violet Elizabeth, sweetly, 'ith me.'

'Well, we're going to find you an' take you back.'

'Oh, *pleath*, I don't want to be found and tooken back. I like being with you.'

'Well, we can't keep you about with us all day, can we?' argued William sternly. 'You've gotter go home sometime same as we've gotter go home sometime. Well, we jolly well want our dinner now and we're jolly well going home an' we're jolly well goin' to take you home. He might give us something and . . .'

'All right,' agreed Violet Elizabeth holding up her face, 'if you all kith me I'll be found an' tooken back.'

The four of them stood again before Mr Bott's desk. William and Ginger and Douglas took a step back and Violet Elizabeth took a step forward.

'We've found her,' said William.

'Where?' said Mr Bott looking round.

'Ith me,' piped Violet Elizabeth.

Mr Bott started.

'You?' he repeated in amazement.

'Yeth, father, ith me.'

'But, but – God bless my soul . . .' he ejaculated peering at the unfamiliar apparition. 'It's impossible.'

Then he rang for Violet Elizabeth's nurse.

'Is this Violet Elizabeth?' he said.

'Yeth, ith me,' said Violet Elizabeth again.

Violet Elizabeth's nurse pushed back the tangle of hair.

'Oh, the poor child!' she cried. 'The poor child!'

'God bless my soul,' said Mr Bott again. 'Take her away. I don't know what you do to her, but do it and don't let her mother see her till it's done, and you boys stay here.'

'Oh, my lamb!' sobbed Violet Elizabeth's nurse as she led her away. 'My poor lamb!'

In an incredibly short time they returned. The mysterious something had been done. Violet Elizabeth's head was a mass of curls. Her face shone with cleanliness. Dainty lace-trimmed skirts stuck out ballet-dancer-wise beneath the pale blue waistband. Mr Bott took a deep breath.

'Now fetch her mother,' he said.

Like a tornado entered Mrs Bott. She still heaved with hysterics. She enfolded Violet Elizabeth to her visibly palpitating bosom.

'My child,' she sobbed. 'Oh my darling child.'

'I wath a thquaw,' said Violet Elizabeth. 'It dothn't make any thort of a noith. Ith a lady.'

'How did you ...' began Mrs Bott still straining Violet Elizabeth to her.

'These boys found her ...' said Mr Bott.

'Oh, how kind – how noble,' said Mrs Bott. 'And one's that nice little boy who played with her so sweetly yesterday. Give them ten shillings each, Botty.'

'Well, but ...' hesitated Mr Bott remembering the circumstances in which they had been brought to him.

'Botty!' screamed Mrs Bott tearfully, 'don't you value your darling child's life at even thirty shillings?'

Hastily Mr Bott handed them each a ten-shilling note.

They tramped homewards by the road.

'Well, it's turned out all right,' said Ginger lugubriously, but fingering the ten-shilling note in his pocket, 'but it might not have. 'Cept for the money it jolly well spoilt the morning.'

'Girls always do,' said William. 'I'm not going to have anything to do with any ole girl ever again.'

''S all very well sayin' that,' said Douglas who had been deeply impressed that morning by the inevitableness and deadly persistence of the sex, ''s all very well sayin' that. It's them what has to do with you.'

'An' I'm never goin' to marry any ole girl,' said William.

''S all very well sayin *that*,' said Douglas again gloomily, 'but some ole girl'll probably marry you.'

THE PRIME OF MISS JEAN BRODIE

(AN EXTRACT)

◆

Muriel Spark

Sandy Stranger had a feeling at the time that they were supposed to be the happiest days of her life, and on her tenth birthday she said so to her best friend Jenny Gray who had been asked to tea at Sandy's house. The speciality of the feast was pineapple cubes with cream, and the speciality of the day was that they were left to themselves. To Sandy the unfamiliar pineapple had the authentic taste and appearance of happiness and she focused her small eyes closely on the pale gold cubes before she scooped them up in her spoon, and she thought the sharp taste on her tongue was that of a special happiness, which was nothing to do with eating, and was different from the happiness of play that one enjoyed unawares. Both girls saved the cream to the last, then ate it in spoonfuls.

'Little girls, you are going to be the *crème de la crème*,' said Sandy, and Jenny spluttered her cream into her handkerchief.

'You know,' Sandy said, 'these are supposed to be the happiest days of our lives.'

'Yes, they are always saying that,' Jenny said. 'They say, make the most of your schooldays because you never know what lies ahead of you.'

'Miss Brodie says prime is best,' Sandy said.

'Yes, but she never got married like our mothers and fathers.'

'They don't have primes,' said Sandy.

'They have sexual intercourse,' Jenny said.

The little girls paused, because this was still a stupendous thought, and one which they had only lately lit upon; the very phrase and its meaning were new. It was quite unbelievable. Sandy said, then, 'Mr Lloyd had a baby last week. He must have committed sex with his wife.' This idea was easier to cope with and they laughed screamingly into their pink paper napkins. Mr Lloyd was the Art master to the Senior girls.

'Can you *see* it happening?' Jenny whispered.

Sandy screwed her eyes even smaller in the effort of seeing with her mind. 'He would be wearing his pyjamas,' she whispered back.

The girls rocked with mirth, thinking of one-armed Mr Lloyd, in his solemnity, striding into school.

Then Jenny said, 'You do it on the spur of the moment. That's how it happens.'

Jenny was a reliable source of information, because a girl employed by her father in his grocer shop had recently been found to be pregnant, and Jenny had picked up some fragments of the ensuing fuss. Having confided her finds to Sandy, they had embarked on a course of research which they called 'research', piecing together clues from remembered conversations illicitly overheard, and passages from the big dictionaries.

'It all happens in a flash,' Jenny said. 'It happened to Teenie when she was out walking at Puddocky with her boy friend. Then they had to get married.'

'You would think the urge would have passed by the time she got her *clothes* off,' Sandy said. By 'clothes' she definitely meant to imply knickers, but 'knickers' was rude in this scientific context.

'Yes, that's what I can't understand,' said Jenny.

Sandy's mother looked round the door and said, 'Enjoying yourselves, darlings?' Over her shoulder appeared the head of Jenny's mother. 'My word,' said Jenny's mother, looking at the tea-table, 'they've been tucking in!'

Sandy felt offended and belittled by this; it was as if the main idea of the party had been the food.

'What would you like to do now?' Sandy's mother said.

Sandy gave her mother a look of secret ferocity which meant: you promised to leave us all on our own, and a promise is a promise, you know it's very bad to break a promise to a child, you might ruin all my life by breaking your promise, it's my birthday.

Sandy's mother backed away bearing Jenny's mother with her. 'Let's leave them to themselves,' she said. 'Just enjoy yourselves, darlings.'

Sandy was sometimes embarrassed by her mother being English and calling her 'darling', not like the mothers of Edinburgh who said 'dear'. Sandy's mother had a flashy winter coat trimmed with fluffy fox fur like the Duchess of York's, while the other mothers wore tweed or, at the most, musquash that would do them all their days.

It had been raining and the ground was too wet for them to go and finish digging the hole to Australia, so the girls lifted the tea-table with all its festal relics over to the corner of the room. Sandy opened the lid of the piano stool and extracted a notebook from between two sheaves of music. On the first page of the notebook was written:

The Mountain Eyrie
by
Sandy Stranger and Jenny Gray

This was a story, still in the process of composition, about Miss Brodie's lover, Hugh Carruthers. He had not been killed in the war, that was a mistake in the telegram. He had come back from the war and called to inquire for Miss Brodie at school, where the first person whom he encountered was Miss Mackay, the headmistress. She had informed him that Miss Brodie did not desire to see him, she loved another. With a bitter, harsh laugh, Hugh went and made his abode in a mountain eyrie, where, wrapped in a leather jacket, he had been discovered one day by Sandy and Jenny. At the present stage in the story Hugh was holding Sandy captive but Jenny had escaped by night and was attempting to find her way down the mountainside in the dark. Hugh was preparing to pursue her.

Sandy took a pencil from a drawer in the sideboard and continued:

'Hugh!' Sandy beseeched him, 'I swear to you before all I hold sacred that Miss Brodie has never loved another, and she awaits you below, praying and hoping in her prime. If you will let Jenny go, she will bring back your lover Jean Brodie to you and you will see her with your own eyes and hold her in your arms after these twelve long years and a day.'

His black eye flashed in the lamplight of the hut. 'Back, girl!' he cried, 'and do not bar my way. Well do I know that yon girl Jenny will report my whereabouts to my mocking erstwhile fiancée. Well do I know that you are both spies sent by her that she might mock. Stand back from the door, I say!'

'Never!' said Sandy, placing her young lithe body squarely in front of the latch and her arm through the bolt. Her large eyes flashed with an azure light of appeal.

Sandy handed the pencil to Jenny. 'It's your turn,' she said.

Jenny wrote: With one movement he flung her to the farthest end of the hut and strode out into the moonlight and his strides made light of the drifting snow.

'Put in about his boots,' said Sandy.

Jenny wrote: His high boots flashed in the moonlight.

'There are too many moonlights,' Sandy said, 'but we can sort that later when it comes to publication.'

'Oh, but it's a secret, Sandy!' said Jenny.

'I know that,' Sandy said. 'Don't worry, we won't publish it till our prime.'

'Do you think Miss Brodie ever had sexual intercourse with Hugh?' said Jenny.

'She would have had a baby, wouldn't she?'

'I don't know.'

'I don't think they did anything like that,' said Sandy. 'Their love was above all that.'

'Miss Brodie said they clung to each other with passionate abandon on his last leave.'

'I don't think they took their clothes off, though,' Sandy said, 'do you?'

'No. I can't see it,' said Jenny.

'I wouldn't like to have sexual intercourse,' Sandy said.

'Neither would I. I'm going to marry a pure person.'

'Have a toffee.'

They ate their sweets, sitting on the carpet. Sandy put some coal on the fire and the light spurted up, reflecting on Jenny's ringlets. 'Let's be witches by the fire, like we were at Hallowe'en.'

They sat in the twilight eating toffees and incanting witches' spells. Jenny said, 'There's a Greek god at the museum standing up with nothing on. I saw it last Sunday afternoon but I was with Auntie Kate and I didn't have a chance to *look* properly.'

'Let's go to the museum next Sunday,' Sandy said. 'It's research.'

'Would you be allowed to go alone with me?'

Sandy, who was notorious for not being allowed to go out and about without a grown-up person, said, 'I don't think so. Perhaps we could get someone to take us.'

'We could ask Miss Brodie.'

Miss Brodie frequently took the little girls to the art galleries and museums, so this seemed feasible.

'But suppose,' said Sandy, 'she won't let us look at the statue if it's naked.'

'I don't think she would notice that it was naked,' Jenny said. 'She just wouldn't see its thingummyjig.'

'I know,' said Sandy. 'Miss Brodie's above all that.'

LOVE IN A COLD CLIMATE

(AN EXTRACT)

───────────── ♦ ─────────────

Nancy Mitford

Polly handed Lady Montdore a cup of tea and told her my news. The happy afterglow from her royal outing immediately faded, and she became intensely disagreeable.

'Engaged?' she said. 'Well, I suppose that's very nice. Alfred what did you say? Who is he? What is that name?'

'He's a don, at Oxford.'

'Oh, dear, how extraordinary. You don't want to go and live at Oxford, surely? I should think he had better go into politics and buy a place – I suppose he hasn't got one by the way? No, or he wouldn't be a don, not an English don at least, in Spain of course, it's quite different – dons are somebody there, I believe. Let's think – yes, why shouldn't your father give you a place as a wedding present? You're the only child he's ever likely to have. I'll write to him at once – where is he now?'

I said vaguely that I believed in Jamaica, but did not know his address.

'Really, what a family! I'll find out from the Colonial Office and write by bag, that will be safest. Then this Mr Thing can settle down and write books. It always gives a man status if he writes a book, Fanny, I advise you to start him off on that immediately.'

'I'm afraid I haven't much influence with him,' I said uneasily.

'Oh, well, develop it dear, quick. No use marrying a man you can't influence. Just look what I've done for Montdore, always seen that he takes an interest, made him accept things (jobs, I mean) and kept him up to the mark, never let him slide back. A wife must always be on the look-out, men are so lazy by nature, for example, Montdore is for ever trying to have a little nap in the afternoon, but I won't hear of it, once you begin that, I tell him, you are old, and people who are old find themselves losing interest, dropping out of things and then they might as well be dead. Montdore's only got me to thank if he's not in the same condition as most of his contemporaries, creeping about the Marlborough Club like dying flies and hardly able to drag themselves as far as the House of Lords. I make Montdore walk down there every day. Now, Fanny dear, the more I think of it, the more it seems to me quite ridiculous for you to go marrying a don, what does Emily say?'

'She's awfully pleased.'

'Emily and Sadie are hopeless. You must ask my advice about this sort of thing, I'm very glad indeed you came round, we must think how we can get you out of it. Could you ring him up now and say you've changed your mind, I believe it would be the kindest in the long run to do it that way.'

'Oh, no, I can't.'

'Why not, dear? It isn't in the paper yet.'

'It will be tomorrow.'

'That's where I can be so helpful. I'll send for Geoffrey Dawson now and have it stopped.'

I was quite terrified. 'Please – ' I said, 'oh, please not!'

Polly came to my rescue. 'But she wants to marry him, Mummy, she's in love, and look at her pretty ring!'

Lady Montdore looked, and was confirmed in her opposition. 'That's not a ruby,' she said, as if I had been pretending it was. 'And as for love I should have thought the example of your mother would have taught you something – where has love landed her? Some ghastly white hunter. Love indeed – whoever invented love ought to be shot.'

'Dons aren't a bit the same as white hunters,' said Polly. 'You know how fond Daddy is of them.'

'Oh, I daresay they're all right for dinner, if you like that sort of thing. Montdore does have them over sometimes, I know, but that's no reason why they should go marrying people. So unsuitable, megalomania, I call it. So many people have that, nowadays. No, Fanny, I'm very much distressed.'

'Oh, please don't be,' I said.

'However, if you say it's settled, I suppose there's no more I can do, except to try and help you make a success of it. Montdore can ask the Chief Whip if there's something for you to nurse, that will be best.'

It was on the tip of my tongue to say that what I hoped to be nursing before long would be sent by God and not the Chief Whip, but I restrained myself, nor did I dare to tell her that Alfred was not a Tory.

The conversation now turned upon the subject of my trousseau, about which Lady Montdore was quite as bossy though less embarrassing. I was not feeling much interest in clothes at that time, all my thoughts being of how to decorate and furnish a charming little old house which Alfred had taken me to see after placing the pigeon's egg on my finger, and which, by a miracle of good luck, was to be let.

'The important thing, dear,' she said, 'is to have a really good fur coat, I mean a proper, dark one.' To Lady Montdore, fur meant mink; she could imagine no other kind except sable, but that would be specified. 'Not only will it make all the rest of your clothes look better than they are but you really needn't bother much about anything else as you need never take it off. Above all, don't go wasting money on underclothes, there is nothing stupider – I always borrow Montdore's myself. Now for evening a diamond brooch is a great help, so long as it has good big stones. Oh, dear, when I think of the diamonds your father gave that woman, it really is too bad. All the same, he can't have got through everything, he was enormously rich when he succeeded, I must write to him. Now, dear, we're going to be very practical. No time like the present.'

Roll Me Over, Lay Me Down

Florence King

*T*IME: *1955*
PLACE: *A brand-new salmon-and-gray Chevy.*

The radio was on and Dean Martin, who was a whole octave above whiskey and rye, was singing 'Memories Are Made of This.' My pants were hanging on the gear stick, my garters were pulled askew like crossed eyes. I was trying to figure out when my last period had started, and since I can't count unless I use my fingers, I had to stop playing with Joe Simpson's erection.

I was certain that I had gotten the curse the day after I turned in the term paper on the War of Jenkins's Ear, but I couldn't remember when *that* was. All I knew was that I was sitting in the sorority lounge making up footnotes for the quotations I had invented when Kathleen Hanrahan rushed in screaming that somebody would have to drive her to confession right away because she had just French-kissed with Pat Gilhooly and if she happened to die in the middle of the night she'd go to hell.

Which *must* have been Pat's birthday because Kathleen had been wondering what to give him and we had all recommended a real kiss for a change. So my period must have started two days after that.

Joe Simpson rolled over on top of me. 'Do you want to?'

I screamed as I felt an unmistakable nudge on my bare stomach. 'Don't let any get on me!'

'Let's get in the back!' he panted.

'When is Pat Gilhooly's birthday?'

'What?'

'Because that was two days before my period started and I think it's a bad time because I'm in the middle now and I'm afraid I'll get P.G.'

'Don't worry,' said Joe, reaching for his wallet. 'I've got something.'

'Those things break,' I protested.

'No, they don't. They're tested. It's scientifically imposs-ible. The law of averages . . .'

'I don't want to. I'm a virgin.'

'You don't have anything to worry about, then. A girl can't get P.G. the first time she goes all the way. It's statistically impossible.'

'No, I don't want to. I'm afraid.'

'You little C.T.! You just like to lead a guy on!'

'That's a G.D. lie!'

'Aw, B.S. You're frigid!'

'I am not, you S.O.B! It's just that I'm not that kind of a girl.'

I grabbed my pants, stuffed them in my purse, and re-treated with something less than dignity, because my behind stuck to the leather seat and I had to peel it off with a loud scrape like someone removing a mustard plaster. I rushed like a gazelle into the sorority house so that I could pour Lysol on my stomach before it was too late.

When I entered my room I found my roommate, Lillian Ballinger, sobbing hysterically while Jennie MacPherson tried to comfort her.

'What happened?' I asked.

Jennie bit her lip. 'It got on her.'

Lillian wailed in a higher key, stood up and spread the folds of her voluminous ten-gore skirt.

'Look! How do you get this stuff off? It's like S-N-O-T! I'm P.G., I know it!'

The door burst open, and Pauline Cunningham came in holding a skirt by the tips of her fingers.

'Does anybody have any spot remover? I'm all out.'

Lillian bawled still harder and reached into her pocket for a Kleenex, but pulled out her pants instead. She dried her eyes on them.

'He promised he wouldn't let any get on me, and suddenly it was all over the place!' She looked down in astonishment at her pants under her nose and dropped them with a scream.

Jennie opened her purse. 'Here's a hankie,' she said, except it wasn't. It was her bra. She stared at it, stunned for a moment, then tossed it back in her bag.

'They say if you let it dry you can scrape it off,' Pauline said thoughtfully, eyeing her skirt.

Lillian threw herself down on the bed and kicked her feet in impotent fury.

'I'm P.G., I know it! And he promised!'

Every age has its identifying symbol. The twenties are represented by a ticker tape, the thirties by the Blue Eagle, and the forties by a swastika. To most people, the fifties are summed up nicely by Ike's grin, but to me, the perfect logo for my salad days would be a black taffeta halter-neck cocktail dress covered with semen.

I spent most of the decade suspended in such a state of horniness that every time Joe McCarthy screamed 'Point of order!' all I could think of was a penis, but unfortunately I couldn't do anything about it because I was living in the heyday of the hymen. You didn't have to be Jewish to be Marjorie Morningstar, the only penetrated hole was the one in Adlai Stevenson's shoe, and anyone who talked about bangs meant Mamie's hair style.

When the fifties opened, the two watchwords that were constantly dinned into us were, 'Stay as sweet as you are,' which was ideally somewhere between Jeanne Crain and June

Allyson, and, 'What will you say when you get married?' which our mothers screamed at us as they locked up their Tampax supply after catching us reading the brochure.

The hymen obsessed everyone, though it was never called by its proper name. It was referred to as your *innocence*, your *purity*, your *goodness*, your *maidenhead*, your *mark*, as in *mark of Cain*, and your *shield*, which never failed to make me think about the picture of the dead Spartan soldier in my history book. *Dulce et decorum est* not to get laid. We were told that 'Men can tell' and warned not to wipe ourselves too hard, which led to untold confusion about the logistics of sexual congress. We were told everything about the hymen except where it is, what it is, and the whimsical fact that the human female shares this pearl beyond price with no other species of living creature except the elephant, the ass, and the pig.

Like Diogenes in search of one honest man, I spent an inordinate amount of time locked in the bathroom searching for my hymen. Though we were not allowed to wear any makeup except a little pink lipstick, at about age thirteen or so, most of us received the gift of a compact to make us feel grown up. These compacts seldom saw reflections of a shiny nose because we were too busy steaming up the mirrors with our genitals during our look-see reconnaissance sessions on the toilet.

With the heraldic tables in *Burke's Peerage* firmly in mind, I probed carefully for my shield, hoping that I had not wiped myself hard enough to produce a bend sinister on what my future husband would expect to find *engoulé gardant*. I searched high and low – literally – but there was nothing sufficiently steely and unequivocal.

I was terrified that I had somehow ruined myself for marriage when I noticed the clitoris. I didn't know it was a clitoris; I referred to it as the Bump, but as I studied its reflection in my compact, everything became clear. *This* was the famous maidenhead! It had to be; it was the only thing I could find that looked like a little head. I felt much better then, scratched out the first draft of the suicide note that I had inadvertently written on the back of my Latin homework, and called my girl friend to tell her about my discovery. 'You know the bump? Well, intercourse,' I said, 'is when the man presses the bump with his thing and then the bump falls off.'

I stuck to my clitoral theory for very good and logical reasons, I thought, because every time I got hot, I noticed a very pleasant, tickly sort of itch in my Bump. This proved beyond a doubt that I was right, after all, and I told my girl friend about it. 'Itching,' I said, 'is when you want a man to do it to you. If the bump is the part that feels good, that must be where it happens,' little knowing that twenty years later an organization called Women's Lib would be saying something similar.

Then a movie called *The Great Caruso* came out, and I went into heat with headlong, wanton abandon. One night I started humping the loose spring in my mattress and pretending it was Mario Lanza. I was fifteen, and from that moment on, I harbored a conscious desire for sex, which, in the fifties, was like harboring a conscious desire for the Hope diamond or a true chip off the old rugged cross.

As things turned out, I ended up being deflowered in the doctor's office, where the light finally dawned.

I had been suffering for some time from severe menstrual cramps, and usually fainted once every period. My mother took me to the doctor, who said that in order to make a thorough examination, he would have to 'break through.' He patted my shoulder, then offered my mother a seat when she started to cry, and told us not to worry because he would give me a certificate of virginity.

'She can show it to her husband when she marries,' he explained. 'That way, he'll know that he didn't get damaged goods.'

I nearly took a flying dive out of his office window because I was certain that my mark of purity was now a mark of the bed spring. When he cut off my bump, he would realize that I had 'done something to myself,' would refuse to issue a certificate, and then – what? My mother would have a fit, that's what, and my father would get That Look on his face, the same look he always got when he turned the pages of my baby book, the same look he got the day I started to menstruate. Then, when he recovered, he would do *something*; I wasn't quite sure what, but being sued for restitution of my allowance was one thing that passed through my terrified brain.

The next day I climbed into the stirrups and put my arms over my eyes in resignation while the doctor froze the area and started snipping away. I couldn't imagine what he was doing way down where he was because he was nowhere near The Bump. At last he said, 'That's got it,' and stuck his finger in me, whereupon I exclaimed, 'Oh! Now I get it!'

'How's that, honey?' he muttered.

'Er, nothing.'

He patted my foot, shook his head, told me to drink lots of hot tea, using a heating pad, and avoid getting my feet wet. 'There's one thing that really cures cramps, and that's having a baby,' he informed me, patting my bare foot again. 'Now you stay as sweet as you are, honey. Here's your certificate.'

It was most impressive except that it started out with 'To Whom It May Concern,' which sounded ominously like a collective summons to the Seventh Fleet, and it bore a notary's seal, since his nurse was so endowed. When we got home my mother announced that I had a certificate of virginity. By this time, the walls of our living room were covered with my certificates; I had one for every honor society and accelerated course imaginable, and my father had proudly framed them all. As soon as he heard the key word *certificate*, he automatically started poking around in his tool chest for nails and wire until my mother stopped him. My grandmother, who did not believe in intellectual women, snorted and said: 'Well, she's got a piece of paper for everything else, she might as well have one for that.'

I entered college in 1953 at the age of seventeen. My introduction to campus life was a picnic during orientation week at which the boys sat on one side of the grove and the girls sat on the other while we sang 'Roll Me Over, Lay Me Down, and Do It Again,' punctuated by salvos of giggles and/or guffaws, depending upon which side of the grove you were on. The only real cruising that took place was intra-sexual, as the sorority and fraternity wigs looked over the freshman class.

My sexual frustration would have been unbearable except that, like all fifties co-eds, I visualized automatic marriage at twenty-one along with voting and legal booze. As we all well knew, 'men might run around with bad girls, but they don't marry them,' so we were willing to wait four years for a lifetime of simultaneous orgasms three times a week, which is what all the manuals promised us. We did not doubt for a moment that the wedding march would follow on the heels of 'Pomp and Circumstance,' preferably within the same week. This was known as Finding Somebody, and we considered it our birthright. I fantasized myself floating out of the bathroom in a white negligee saying 'Here, read this' to a nebulous bridegroom with an ascot around the neck of his silk dressing gown, but meanwhile I wanted all the permissible fun I could get short of Going All the Way.

In high school I had done nothing but kiss, so when I got to college I was determined to find out what 'the other things' felt like. In other words, I wanted to do Everything But, sometimes known as Making Out. Our mothers warned us against this practice, saying 'A boy will go as far as a girl will let him' and 'He's just testing you.'

Since we all wanted to be tested as much as possible, we had to draw up unwritten laws for our ostensibly illegal activities, like Mississippi's famous 'black-market tax' on illegal liquor.

With a talent for partitioning unrivaled since the Congress

of Vienna, we divided ourselves into a rigidly classified set of love play areas known as Above the Waist, or Up Top; Below the Waist, or There; and finally that *casus belli* that masqueraded under the *nom de guerre* of Inside Me.

French-kissing was no big deal; everybody did that except Kathleen Hanrahan, who used to kiss Pat Gilhooly through a handkerchief. The first real *pas de deux* that had to be negotiated was Above the Waist/Over the Clothes, or, Beginning Petting.

My first venture into this field occurred with Jack Garrett, who asked me for a date as we bent over the formaldehyde vat in zoology lab fishing out our foetal pigs.

In keeping with the partitioning rules, I had to wait three dates – a total of three weeks – before I got my bust fondled. I couldn't permit even a kiss on the first date; on the second I was able to allow a long but dry buss, and on the third date it was okay to neck in the car, which included French-kissing, and if the girl didn't pull away it was a signal that the boy could Go Further.

It seemed to me that I waited an interminable length of time to get what I wanted. We French-kissed through three verses each of 'O Mein Papa,' 'Hernando's Hideaway,' and 'The Barefoot Contessa.' Since the latter was the theme of a movie about a man who didn't have a penis, I began to wonder if Ava Gardner and I had a penchant for eunuchs.

Finally, I felt the hand creep up, whereupon the strains of 'Papa Loves Mambo' were drowned out by the fortissimo crackle of my taffeta bodice. We might as well have shaken hands because I didn't feel a thing. Besides the taffeta dress, I was wearing a bra with circular-stitched cups to achieve that collie-muzzle point so popular in the fifties, plus camisole-style slip.

Jack didn't try to go further, so I gave it up as a bad job and said, 'I think I'd better go in now,' which meant Stop. The next day in zoo lab, he steadfastly refused to look at me, which wasn't surprising because he dropped his pig and splashed formaldehyde in his eyes.

I tried Above the Waist/Over the Clothes a few more times, taking care to wear something a little more suited to such abandoned intimacy, but even my most wanton bra had lined cups and enough lace to outfit the Pope for Easter Sunday high mass. Obviously, this stage of making out was comparable to something the boys referred to as 'washing your feet with your socks on,' so I decided to press on to Above the Waist/Under the Clothes, or Intermediate Petting.

According to unofficial sorority ground rules, this practice had to be initiated on a special occasion, a 'big date' such as a semiformal frat party. In a mood of cynical premeditation which I chose to call common sense, I wore a strapless bra that I could merely unhook and toss aside. However, since it was a semiformal affair, I had to wear a cocktail dress, and since it was 1954, all my cocktail dresses had halter necklines.

That was the night I almost hung myself. The halter neckline was everyone's nemesis and nearly caused several bizarre mishaps, but I set an unchallenged record for insuperable conundrums by turning into a Chinese puzzle in the front seat of Pete Farrington's car.

Pete had been rubbing my bare back long enough to discover the zipper in my dress. He lowered the tab, and I made ready to slip the yoke over my head, which would have allowed the dress to fall conveniently off the entire top half of me. I had my head halfway through the halter when Pete, overcome with lust, grabbed my bra and, instead of unhooking it, followed my example and yanked it up and around my neck in an attempt to pull it over my head. The bra caught me under the chin, mumps fashion, the dress got stuck on my earrings, my hair ended up in my mouth, and I scratched my nose on my sorority pin. Pete tried to remedy matters by twisting the bra to free it, a solution somewhat akin to using the albatross as a tourniquet. I ended up jack-knifed forward, tossing and jerking my head like a horse wearing a martingale.

Pete leaned over and said, 'Are you all right?' at which precise and sublime moment, the car door opened and I had the first of my many compromising encounters with Ira the Terrible, the campus warden.

Ira was a retired cop who roamed around looking for cars without any heads in them. His rule of thumb was to bypass any car in which he could see two heads, more or less side by side in the *front* seat. If you slid down below window level, or if he saw you in the back, he would yank open the door, shine his flashlight in and say, needlessly, 'What's going on here?'

I felt a blast of cold air, then the car was flooded with light and Ira's gravelly voice started barking out questions.

'What's going on here? What're you kids up to? What in the hell is wrong with *her*?'

'She . . . had an accident,' Pete mumbled.

'Sit up, girlie!' Ira ordered, and tapped me on my bare back, with his icy flashlight. I gurgled out a yell.

'I can't move!'

'What didya do to her, buddy?'

'I didn't do anything,' Pete said in a quavering voice. 'She must have pulled a muscle.'

'Yeah? A muscle in her *what*? Look here, girlie, you can't stay like that all night. Where do you live? Start that car, buddy, I'm escortin' the two of you back to her dorm.'

The next time I wore a cardigan sweater and a strapless bra and successfully negotiated Above the Waist/Under the Clothes. After doing this with a number of different dates and comparing notes with my sorority sisters, I had reason to believe that the boys had their unofficial ground rules, too. Invariably, when you unveiled yourself they would stare pop-eyed at you and gasp, 'God, they're beautiful!' This was a set piece that never varied, as standard a line as Helen Trent's 'We can't go on like this.'

After the recitativo, they took a flying lunge and grabbed handfuls of flesh with such ferocity that they almost knocked you out of the car. They either didn't know about nipple power or they didn't care; in keeping with the belle idea of the era, their main interest was cleavage, as in Marilyn Monroe, Diana Dors, and Zsa Zsa Gabor. If you didn't have a natural cleavage, they squeezed you together until one formed, then sat there and stared at it.

Getting one's nipples kissed, or as we genteelly put it, 'He kissed me up top,' resulted in hideous purple and green bruises that we called hickeys. Providing the housemother was out of earshot, we spied on one another and when we caught sight of one, we shrieked, 'Ooooh! Shirley's got a hick-eee, Shirley's got a hick-eee,' followed by a hysterical salvo of giggles.

Physiology being what it is, the first time I wet-nursed, I met Ira again because Wade Griffiths slid down in the seat the better to reach me with. Suddenly the door burst open and there was Ira with his blinding *flambeau*.

'All right, you kids, straighten up and fly right. Start that motor, buddy, I'm escortin' you back to her dorm.'

Below the Waist/There, or intimate fingering, was serious business reserved for a boy you were practically going steady with. It was considered a good way to round off a really special date, such as a formal dance; consequently, you almost got smothered to death because yards and yards of material came flying up in your face. Flounced tulle, linings, underskirts, petticoats, crinolines, and a six-tier steel hoop. When you finally got your pudenda excavated, the next problem was negotiating a garment known as a Merry Widow, or, as we sometimes called it, the Iron Maiden. It was a combination half-cup strapless bra, waist-pincher, girdle, garter belt, and pants, all in one. It was constructed of black lace over black satin over starched canvas and reinforced with fifteen strips of steel. It tended to amputate the wearer at the hip, leave deep red welts, cut off all circulation in the legs, and maintained a constant threat of spontaneous circumcision because it had a detachable crotch piece that rode up the middle of your vulva and girted you within an inch of your life.

However, the crotch piece was very convenient for heavy petting because all one needed to do was unsnap four snaps and *voilà*. After you finished, it fit into an evening bag without any telltale bulges, unlike full-fledged pants. Always, after a big dance, the laundry room in the sorority house sported a wall-to-wall clothesline full of drying crotch pieces.

Some of the boys knew about the clitoris and some did not, but even the most enlightened sports were so used to masturbating themselves in hearty male fashion that they rubbed me raw. One date actually started slapping me with his palm. There was a set script to fingering, too. As soon as he touched it and felt the lubrication he would say, 'You're passionate, aren't you?' Of course you didn't dare say yes because that was an extremely dangerous word to toss around in the fifties. Maidenly prudence was served by a shuddery sigh, whereupon the boy gasped and said, 'Oh, God!'

Once the game was afoot, you had to concentrate on trying to keep his finger in the right place while you both kept one eye peeled for Ira. To the accompaniment of telltale oleaginous sounds the deathless dialogue was recited:

'Here?'
'Higher!'
'There?'
'Lighter!'
'Like this?'
'Up top!'
'Does that feel good?'
'Lower!'
'More?'
'Higher!'
'Like that?'
'Right there! Oh, right there!'
'Do you like that?'
'Oh, don't stop! Don't stop!'

'I think I hear Ira.'

A girl wearing four-inch spike heels and having a climax in the front seat of a car can do a lot of damage. There were an awful lot of broken heaters; Lillian Ballinger stripped the gears once and Jennie MacPherson put her foot through the windshield, but once again I walked away with the honors and straight into campus legend.

It was the night of the spring formal, and Joe Simpson had found the right place for a change. When I climaxed, I jerked as though I had sat on a live wire. My feet flew up and somehow, some way, my heel got caught in the horn rim. The horn blasted away, and as I struggled to free myself, it got stuck. I panicked and twisted my ankle under the steering wheel in an effort to get untangled, and a numbing pain shot up my leg. I yelled bloody murder and buried Joe Simpson under a cascade of flounced tulle, linings, underskirts, petticoats, crinoline, and my six-tier steel hoop. By this time I was practically standing on my head and my legs were splayed out as far as they would stretch. The noise brought Ira out of the bull rushes with his flashlight at charge. He yanked open the door, rammed the torch in and hit me right in the bare crotch.

'What's going on here!'

'The horn's stuck,' Joe yelled.

'*I'm* stuck!'

Ira ran to the hood, threw it open, and yanked at the wires. The noise cut off but I was unable to repair my dignity because I was paralyzed. Ira peered in, then quickly turned his back.

'Cover yourself, girlie.'

By twisting out of my shoe, rolling over onto my stomach and doing something flappy that vaguely resembled the Australian crawl, I got free.

'All right,' I signaled, and Ira turned around.

'Oh, no,' he muttered. 'It's you again.' He stuck his flashlight into his belt and jerked his thumb in the direction of the sorority houses.

'Start that motor, buddy, and follow me.'

If nothing untoward happened, fingering always ended with a breathless and somewhat awed male question: 'Did I make you happy?' No one ever said *come*. The accepted reply to this peerless euphemism was another peerless euphemism: 'Something happened to me.' It was also okay to gasp, while you were kicking a hole in the heater or demolishing the dashboard, 'It's happening!'

Then it was all over but the shooting – literally. Satisfying the boys was something we did with the utmost reluctance because we were all scared dreckless of sperm. If it got *on* you, anywhere *near* you, you *could* get pregnant, it *had* happened. A sheaf of horror stories made the rounds of the sorority, all about girls who got pregnant in swimming pools because a boy had ejaculated near them, and one chilling tale of woe about the New York water shortage and the girl who, in a spirit of civic responsibility, had used her brother's bath water after him.

As a result, we seldom masturbated the boys. We satisfied them by letting them rub against us. In the frat house we let them get on top of us but in cars it was done side by side, frontal view. To be on the safe side, we always put our pants back on and pulled our skirts down. When the boys started to go stiff and tremble we screamed, 'Don't let it get on me!' and pulled away with all the strength we could muster.

The man who ran the dry cleaning shop drove a Cadillac. Sometimes the boys managed to get their flies open on time and finished on the floor, while we plastered ourselves against the door and pulled our feet out of the way. Edith Whitmore was scared silly of even being in the car when it happened, and one night she ran all the way up to the gym.

I masturbated a boy for the first time while sloshed to the gills during our senior year Homecoming dance. This was an almost insurmountable problem in the dressy fifties because I was wearing eighteen-inch white kid gloves that fit like skin. Once you got them on, which took twenty minutes per hand, you couldn't get them off again, but fortunately the manufacturer had had the foresight to include six little pearl buttons on the insides of the wrists so that ladies could drink, smoke, go to the bathroom, and, presumably, masturbate their dates at formal dances.

By this time I was sick of partitioning and divvying up the various portions of myself in the mad ballet of Making Out. I started to feel a little schizy around the edges; it became eerily like the Treaty of Versailles, with one of my breasts awarded to Greece and the other awarded to Turkey, and access to my vagina weighed as if it were a kind of Dardanelles. I got fed up, decided to write thirty to the whole business, and lost my virginity with the aid of two rubbers, three Norforms, coitus interruptus, and a douche.

I didn't get P.G.

THE SECRET DIARY OF ADRIAN MOLE AGED 13 $\frac{3}{4}$

(AN EXTRACT)

———————————— ♦ ————————————

Sue Townsend

Thursday January 1st
BANK HOLIDAY IN ENGLAND,
IRELAND, SCOTLAND AND WALES.

These are my New Year's resolutions:
1 I will help the blind across the road.
2 I will hang my trousers up.
3 I will put the sleeves back on my records.
4 I will not start smoking.
5 I will stop squeezing my spots.
6 I will be kind to the dog.
7 I will help the poor and ignorant.
8 After hearing the disgusting noises from downstairs last night, I have also vowed never to drink alcohol.

My father got the dog drunk on cherry brandy at the party last night. If the RSPCA hear about it he could get done. Eight days have gone since Christmas Day but my mother still hasn't worn the green lurex apron I bought her for Christmas! She will get bathcubes next year.

Just my luck, I've got a spot on my chin for the first day of the New Year!

————————————

Friday January 2nd
BANK HOLIDAY IN SCOTLAND. FULL MOON.

I felt rotten today. It's my mother's fault for singing 'My Way' at two o'clock in the morning at the top of the stairs. Just my luck to have a mother like her. There is a chance my parents could be alcoholics. Next year I could be in a children's home.

The spot on my chin is getting bigger. It's my mother's fault for not knowing about vitamins.

Saturday January 3rd

I shall go mad through lack of sleep! My father has banned the dog from the house so it barked outside my window all night. Just my luck! My father shouted a swear-word at it. If he's not careful he will get done by the police for obscene language.

I think the spot is a boil. Just my luck to have it where everybody can see it. I pointed out to my mother that I hadn't had any vitamin C today. She said: 'Go and buy an orange, then.' This is typical.

She still hasn't worn the lurex apron.

I will be glad to get back to school.

Thursday January 8th

Now my mother has got the flu. This means that I have to look after them both. Just my luck!

I have been up and down the stairs all day. I cooked a big dinner for them tonight: two poached eggs with beans, and tinned semolina pudding. (It's a good job I wore the green lurex apron because the poached eggs escaped out of the pan and got all over me.) I nearly said something when I saw they hadn't eaten *any* of it. They can't be that ill. I gave it to the dog in the coal shed. My grandmother is coming tomorrow morning, so I had to clean the burnt saucepans, then take the dog for a walk. It was half-past eleven before I got to bed. No wonder I am short for my age.

I have decided against medicine for a career.

Tuesday January 13th

My father has gone back to work. Thank God! I don't know how my mother sticks him.

Mr Lucas came in this morning to see if my mother needed any help in the house. He is very kind. Mrs Lucas was next door cleaning the outside windows. The ladder didn't look very safe. I have written to Malcolm Muggeridge, c/o the BBC, asking him what to do about being an intellectual. I hope he writes back soon because I'm getting fed up being one on my own. I have written a poem, and it only took me two minutes. Even the famous poets take longer than that. It is called 'The Tap', but it isn't really about a tap, it's very deep, and about life and stuff like that.

> *The Tap, by Adrian Mole*
> The tap drips and keeps me awake,
> In the morning there will be a lake.
> For the want of a washer the carpet will spoil,
> Then for another my father will toil.
> My father could snuff it while he is at work.
> Dad, fit a washer don't be a burk!

I showed it to my mother, but she laughed. She isn't very bright. She still hasn't washed my PE shorts, and it is school tomorrow. She is not like the mothers on television.

Wednesday January 14th

Joined the library. Got *Care of the Skin*, *Origin of Species*, and a book by a woman my mother is always going on about. It is called *Pride and Prejudice*, by a woman called Jane Austen. I could tell the librarian was impressed. Perhaps she is an intellectual like me. She didn't look at my spot, so perhaps it is getting smaller. About time!

Mr Lucas was in the kitchen drinking coffee with my mother. The room was full of smoke. They were laughing, but when I went in, they stopped.

Mrs Lucas was next door cleaning the drains. She looked as if she was in a bad mood. I think Mr and Mrs Lucas have got an unhappy marriage. Poor Mr Lucas!

None of the teachers at school have noticed that I am an intellectual. They will be sorry when I am famous. There is a new girl in our class. She sits next to me in Geography. She is all right. Her name is Pandora, but she likes being called 'Box'. Don't ask me why. I might fall in love with her. It's time I fell in love, after all I am 13¾ years old.

Thursday January 15th

Pandora has got hair the colour of treacle, and it's long like girls' hair should be. She has got quite a good figure. I saw her playing netball and her chest was wobbling. I felt a bit funny. I think this is it!

The dog has had its stitches out. It bit the vet, but I expect he's used to it. (The vet I mean; I know the dog is.)

My father found out about the arm on the stereo. I told a lie. I said the dog jumped up and broke it. My father said he will wait until the dog is completely cured of its operation then kick it. I hope this is a joke.

Mr Lucas was in the kitchen again when I got home from school. My mother is better now, so why he keeps coming round is a mystery to me. Mrs Lucas was planting trees in the dark. I read a bit of *Pride and Prejudice*, but it was very old-fashioned. I think Jane Austen should write something a bit more modern.

The dog has got the same colour eyes as Pandora. I only noticed because my mother cut the dog's hair. It looks worse than ever. Mr Lucas and my mother were laughing at the dog's new haircut which is not very nice, because dogs can't answer back, just like the Royal Family.

I am going to bed early to think about Pandora and do my back-stretching exercises. I haven't grown for two weeks. If this carries on I will be a midget.

I will go to the doctor's on Saturday if the spot is still there. I can't live like this with everybody staring.

Friday January 16th

Mr Lucas came round and offered to take my mother shopping in the car. They dropped me off at school. I was glad to get out of the car what with all the laughing and cigarette smoke. We saw Mrs Lucas on the way. She was carrying big bags of shopping. My mother waved, but Mrs Lucas couldn't wave back.

It was Geography today so I sat next to Pandora for a whole hour. She looks better every day. I told her about her eyes being the same as the dog's. She asked what kind of dog it was. I told her it was a mongrel.

I lent Pandora my blue felt-tip pen to colour round the British Isles.

I think she appreciates these small attentions.

I started *Origin of Species* today, but it's not as good as the television series. *Care of the Skin* is dead good. I have left it open on the pages about vitamins. I hope my mother takes the hint. I have left it on the kitchen table near the ashtray, so she is bound to see it.

I have made an appointment about the spot. It has turned purple.

Monday January 19th

I have joined a group at school called the Good Samaritans. We go out into the community helping and stuff like that. We miss Maths on Monday afternoons.

Today we had a talk on the sort of things we will be doing. I have been put in the old age pensioners' group. Nigel has got a dead yukky job looking after kids in a playgroup. He is as sick as a parrot.

I can't wait for next Monday. I will get a cassette so I can tape all the old fogies' stories about the war and stuff. I hope I get one with a good memory.

The dog is back at the vet's. It has got concrete stuck on its paws. No wonder it was making such a row on the stairs last night. Pandora smiled at me in school dinner today, but I was choking on a piece of gristle so I couldn't smile back. Just my luck!

Tuesday January 20th
FULL MOON

My mother is looking for a job!

Now I could end up a delinquent roaming the streets and all that. And what will I do during the holidays? I expect I will have to sit in a launderette all day to keep warm. I will be a latchkey kid, whatever that is. And who will look after the dog? And what will I have to eat all day? I will be forced to eat crisps and sweets until my skin is ruined and my teeth fall out. I think my mother is being very selfish. She won't be any good in a job anyway. She isn't very bright and she drinks too much at Christmas.

I rang my grandma up and told her, and she says I could stay at her house in the holidays, and go to the Evergreens' meetings in the afternoons and stuff like that. I wish I hadn't rung now. The Samaritans met today during break. The old people were shared out. I got an old man called Bert Baxter. He is eighty-nine so I don't suppose I'll have him for long. I'm going round to see him tomorrow. I hope he hasn't got a dog. I'm fed up with dogs. They are either at the vet's or standing in front of the television.

Friday January 23rd

That is the last time I go to a disco. Everybody there was a punk except me and Rick Lemon, the youth leader. Nigel was showing off all night. He ended up putting a safety pin through his ear. My father had to take him to the hospital in our car. Nigel's parents haven't got a car because his father's got a steel plate in his head and his mother is only four feet eleven inches tall. It's not surprising Nigel has turned out bad really, with a maniac and a midget for parents.

I still haven't heard from Malcolm Muggeridge. Perhaps he is in a bad mood. Intellectuals like him and me often have bad moods. Ordinary people don't understand us and say we are sulking, but we're not.

Pandora has been to see Nigel in hospital. He has got a bit of blood poisoning from the safety pin. Pandora thinks Nigel is dead brave. I think he is dead stupid.

I have had a headache all day because of my mother's rotten typing, but I'm not complaining. I must go to sleep now. I've got to go and see Bert Baxter tomorrow at his house. It was the right number WORSE LUCK!

Saturday January 24th

Today was the most terrible day of my life. My mother has got a job doing her rotten typing in an insurance office! She starts on Monday! Mr Lucas works at the same place. He is going to give her a lift every day.

And my father is in a bad mood – he thinks his big-end is going.

But worst of all, Bert Baxter is not a nice old age pensioner! He drinks and smokes and has an alsatian dog called Sabre. Sabre was locked in the kitchen while I was cutting the massive hedge, but he didn't stop growling once.

But even worse than that! Pandora is going out with Nigel!!!!! I think I will never get over this shock.

Sunday January 25th
THIRD AFTER EPIPHANY

10 a.m. I am ill with all the worry, too weak to write much. Nobody has noticed I haven't eaten any breakfast.

2 p.m. Had two junior aspirins at midday and rallied a bit. Perhaps when I am famous and my diary is discovered people will understand the torment of being a 13¾-year-old undiscovered intellectual.

6 p.m. Pandora! My lost love! Now I will never stroke your treacle hair! (Although my blue felt-tip is still at your disposal.)

8 pm. Pandora! Pandora! Pandora!

10 p.m. Why? Why? Why?

Midnight. Had a crab-paste sandwich and a satsuma (for the good of my skin). Feel a bit better. I hope Nigel falls off his bike and is squashed flat by a lorry. I will never speak to him again. He knew I was in love with Pandora! If I'd had a racing bike for Christmas instead of a lousy digital stereo alarm clock, none of this would have happened.

DRUG-CRAZED THUGS WRECKED MY LOUNGE – EXCLUSIVE

Jan Mark

———————— ♦ ————————

'I don't care how much you fancy her,' Nina said. 'I'm not giving you her address.'

'There are ways of finding out,' Maurice said. ''Ve haff ways of making you talk.'

'We even have ways of making you shut up,' Nazzer sighed. 'None of them noticeably successful.'

'You don't want to get involved with Claire, she's Bad News,' Nina said. 'She's trouble.'

'Funny, isn't it,' Maurice said. 'Have you noticed that when you particularly want to do something, some creep always comes along and says, "'You don't want to do that"?'

'What sort of trouble?' Nazzer said. 'If you're trying to put him off, Nina, I don't think you're going the right way about it. If you'd said, "My cousin Claire is beautiful, accomplished, witty, extremely sexy and moreover her legs go all the way to the top," he'd have got very suspicious and demanded to know what was *really* wrong with her.'

'She isn't sexy,' Nina said. 'That's the trouble.'

'I think you might let me find out for myself,' Maurice said. 'I am not particularly inexperienced in these matters.'

'You don't need experience with Claire. You need an interesting book to help pass the time. Look, I *know*,' Nina said. 'I've seen her at home. I went to stay with her just before Easter.'

'Where?'

'Never mind where, you won't be going – no you *won't*, Maurice. Her old man'd never let you over the doorstep for a start.'

'This old man being your uncle? Aha! You've only got one uncle. A simple process of deduction, Watson...'

'Not *that* uncle. He isn't really my uncle anyway. Claire's only a second cousin – I don't know what you'd call him; a sort of uncle twice removed. If he was ten times removed it couldn't be far enough,' Nina said. 'They're a bit old for parents, I mean, they had her late and she's the only one, and they've got this thing about protecting her from corrupting influences.'

'How come they let her knock around with you, then?'

'They don't,' Nina said. 'They reckon that what happened at Easter was all my fault. Well, it was in a way because if I hadn't been there it wouldn't have happened, but it only happened because they let it, it's just that they wouldn't have let it happen if I *hadn't* been there. I mean,' Nina said, 'believe it or not, they don't like going out and leaving her alone in the evening. But they thought the two of us would be safe and sort of extorted promises with menace about not answering the door or the phone.'

'Why not the phone?'

'I dunno. In case there was a man breathing on the other end, I suppose. They've read too many headlines – you know: I WAS A TEENAGE SCHOOLGIRL – EXCLUSIVE.'

'You get these throw-backs,' Nazzer said. 'Think about it; these people must have lived through the swinging sixties. If we are to believe what we hear about the swinging sixties, it was ten years of purple haze with yellow spots. It was rock, surf and acid. It was Liverpool...'

'Mini skirts.'

'Don't you ever think of anything but legs?'

'Tambourines, Chelsea boots, love...'

'Money.'

'Odd about the money. I wonder where it went?'

'My point is,' Nazzer said, 'by all accounts the sixties were something of which you could not remain unaware. They went on for a long time...'

'Almost as long as the seventies.'

'And yet you get these pockets of resistance, people who came through it all absolutely untouched, went into a kind of space warp and leapt from 1959 straight to 1970. I've got this snapshot of my father wearing enormous trousers...'

'He still wears enormous trousers.'

'These were enormous round the turn-ups. And Mum with white lips, looking like a corpse that's had second thoughts, and they still go into embarrassing postures when certain records get played on the radio. It obviously had a lasting effect on them, like the First World War, but there are people, Claire's parents for instance, who behave as though it never happened.'

'I don't think it ever did,' Maurice said. 'I think it was collective hysteria, a sort of mass hallucination, like the Indian Rope Trick. If you credit half of what you see on telly, everyone was hallucinating anyway – including the government,' he added.

'A lot of people say the sixties didn't end till 1970 anyway, like the seventies ended with 1980. There's all these rows about whether the next century starts in the year 2000 or not.'

'This century ends in the year 2000,' Maurice said. 'The next one starts in 2001. The first century started with the year one, didn't it? BC ended with God pressing a button and sending the trip meter back to a row of noughts.'

'Well, all right,' Nina said, 'but Claire's parents were definitely in cold storage during the sixties. They were probably having a private forties revival at the time.'

'Getting in training for the eighties backlash,' Maurice said.

'Well, as soon as Claire's mum and dad had got clear, she sent me down to the corner shop to buy nibbles. She wanted me to try the off-licence, but I wouldn't.'

'For nibbles?'

'For booze.'

'Oh, how noble,' Nazzer said. '"I cannot tell a lie," you said to the salesman. "I am under eighteen".'

'It wasn't that. No one ever asks if I'm eighteen,' Nina said, 'not since I was fourteen. But Claire had asked these guys in from school and I didn't want trouble – not with *her* parents. Claire gets stoned on shandy.'

'Look, I *must* meet her,' Maurice said, urgently. 'This could be a financial breakthrough.'

'That's not what I meant. She could get stoned on cornflakes if she put her mind to it. Soon as I came back with the nibbles I could see something was going on. They've got these cream curtains in the front room, that let the light through, and right down the street I could see the light had turned a sort of dull red. She'd turned off the lamp in the middle and got down all the bedside lights, set out round the edge of the room with red cloth over the shades, what she probably thought was sinful, only the red cloth was a sports shirt and a mini slip and a pink shower cap with a frill. "That'll melt," I said. "We'll have it turned off by the time it gets to melting point," Claire said, and sniggered. Enough to make you puke,' Nina said. 'She'd got all the coffee tables out of their nest and set out those little paté bowls you get from the Co-op – for the nibbles. I'd got olives and cashew nuts, but she had out these wizened sausages on sticks. It all looked a bit dangerous to me.'

'The sausages?'

'No, they just looked nasty. But you couldn't move for bedside lamps, and coffee tables catching you behind the knees. They've got a horrible big glass coffee table too, with bamboo legs, that was up against the wall with a chess set and a row of bottles on it. I said, "Hadn't you better put those away," and she said, "Hell, no, I've only just got them out," sounding really phony. And the drink looked phony too. It wasn't whisky and gin and vodka – well, there was whisky, but the rest was all horrible colours. One of them looked like copper sulphate.'

'Curaçao,' Maurice said. 'It tastes of orange. It's a bit of a shock when you swallow it. I mean, you're *expecting* copper sulphate.'

'And something really foul-looking in a green bottle shaped like a mermaid. I couldn't see which end of the mermaid the drink came out. I started wondering about these fellows she'd invited; Chris and Stu – I'd met them before. I mean, I could imagine what would happen if one of *you* got your hands on that mermaid.'

'It would be creative though,' Nazzer said. 'We wouldn't do anything vulgar, would we, Maurice?'

'We'd got the central heating going full blast, and then Claire put the fire on. It was an electric coal fire, with imitation flickers.'

'I hate those,' Maurice said. 'If you watch long enough you can see the same flicker coming round, over and over again. It must be like a lighthouse inside, only faster.'

'And Claire had draped things all over the settees – scarves and shawls and that, and found about fifteen cushions to sling around. One of them was a pink plush thing and I said, "You'd better put this away," and she said "Why?" and I said, "Because it looks like a fat stomach with a belly button." I didn't fancy Chris or Stu thinking the same thing, half-way through the evening. But Claire just gave this snigger and put the belly cushion right on top of the pile where no one could miss it. I suppose she'd decided to live dangerously.'

'She gets her kicks from cushions?'

'If you had parents like hers, even two thick oafs like Chris and Stu would look dangerous. Well, it was getting on for nine by now, and I thought that if these two didn't turn up soon it would hardly be worth their while turning up at all, because Claire's parents' idea of an evening out is an *evening* out. Evening ends at ten, on their clock. Then it's night. Actually,' Nina said, 'I was hoping they wouldn't come. I could see what Claire had in mind. She had this tiny dress on – I don't know where she'd managed to get anything that small, it may have been a sweater, and she kept stretching, and every time she stretched it got smaller.'

'Look, what's all this *purity* all of a sudden?' Maurice demanded. 'What's all this disapproving of blokes and booze and carnal knowledge?'

'*I* don't mind carnal knowledge,' Nina said. 'I like carnal knowledge. But this was carnal ignorance. Claire looked out through the curtains – that was another stretch and the dress almost disappeared – and there were these two figures in parkas, out in the street, dancing very slowly round a lamp post, knees up, knees up, sort of like Eskimo canni-bals. "What the *hell* are they doing?" says Claire. "Keeping warm?" I said and she said, "Like hell." I could tell,' said Nina, 'that she'd got this idea that Hell is a very bad word. So I said, "Perhaps they're trying to work up courage."

'"*Them* two?" she says – she wouldn't say that normally. She's been brought up to talk *nacely* – "Them two?" she says; "go and tell them to come in," so I said, "You go," and she said, "I'll freeze in this," and sort of shrugged her weeny garment till it got even weenier. "You've got leggings on," she said. "I should take them off later," she said, and made that really nasty noise again, like a smirk, only you could hear it.'

'By the time I got to the door so had they, Chris and Stu. They were leaning on it, and when I turned the catch they fell in on me, Stu did, anyway. Chris fell straight past and hit his head on the banisters. "Well, don't just stand there, come in," says Claire. She was *posing* in the doorway of the lounge and I suppose she had that line already rehearsed. I mean, they *were* in. Chris was so far in he was almost out the back door, but she didn't seem to have noticed. I left them to it and went into the lounge and got a shawl and threw it over the row of bottles. I didn't want to be around afterwards when Claire's dad found out how much was left in them. There was a lot of creaking out in the hall as they took off their parkas . . .'

'*Parkas?*' Nazzer said. 'This is all getting to sound distinctly *quaint*. What were they wearing underneath? Bondage gear?'

'There's nowhere to go but backwards,' Maurice said. 'Bondage gear looked like the end, didn't it?'

'It was,' Nazzer said. 'Nothing's topped it. Personality's down to skin level, now, sort of designer filth.'

'So they all came in and Claire says, "Let's have a drink." She looked very ratty at me and pulled the shawl off the bottles again. Stu said he'd have coffee because he'd got cold hanging about outside and Claire said, "Well, you didn't have to spend half the evening dancing round the lamp post. Have a whisky. It's more warming."

'Stu said, "We got here too early. We thought you might not be ready," and Chris says, "Like not dressed," and laughed, like Claire's smirk, only worse.'

'A kind of audible leer?' Nazzer suggested.

'That's it. So Claire asked *me* to go and make coffee and just as I was going out she said, "What'll you have, Chris?" and I thought, Here we go, because Chris would probably want something inflammatory like a Vodka Cinzano with Ribena, or worse. But he said, "I'll have a coffee too. All me extremities are turning blue and shrunken." I knew what he meant, but she didn't. She misses a lot, really. I said, "What'll you have, Claire?" and she said, "I suppose I'd better have coffee, too." She was really scowling, now, and I nipped out quick before she asked me to make it Irish coffee. Come to think of it,' Nina said, 'I could have given them hot paraffin and Bisto and *told* them it was Irish coffee and they wouldn't have known any different.'

'When I came back with the coffee they were all sitting there looking stuffed. Chris and Stu on one settee and Claire on the other, sort of flirting with the scarf. There wasn't anything else to flirt with.'

'Hang on,' Nazzer said. '*Two* settees? Imitation coal fire? A mermaid? What kind of *ambiance* are these people aiming for?'

'They call them sofas,' Nina explained, 'Claire's parents do. But you can't disguise a settee. It's got settee written all over it.'

'It's that fat middle-aged look they have,' Maurice said, 'Even when they're new.'

'Claire put a record on, disco music, very ancient, only the music centre was behind the settee so all you could hear was a kind of thump thump thump, dead quiet so the neighbours wouldn't hear and come round to grass later, and this thin yelling noise in the background like some tiny mad person was trapped inside the settee and trying to get out. I think it was the only record Claire's got. She must have smuggled it in disguised as a plate. Her mum and dad have got lots but they all seem to be old men singing *I Did it My Way* on one note.'

'Strange how people get this compulsion to sing *I Did it My Way* when they reach a certain age,' Maurice remarked. 'Like they were afraid you might think they hadn't done anything at all.'

'Or else that their way was just like everyone else's so nobody ever noticed them doing it,' Nazzer said. 'It only seems to be men, though. Women don't sing *I Did it My Way*.'

'Claire said, "Have an olive," and Chris said, "With coffee? Have a heart, Hawes." She hates being called Hawes.

She doesn't like the sound of it. "It would be all right with Vermouth," she says, all sophisticated.'

'I thought it was pronounced Ver*mooth*,' Nazzer said. 'Vermouth sounds like a seaside resort.'

'Vermouth rock,' Maurice said.

'"Have a peanut," says Claire. It got very quiet. You could hear peanuts being chewed. I tell you,' Nina said, 'I began to wish that Mr and Mrs Hawes *would* come back, before we all turned to stone. "Have a drink," says Claire, when the peanuts had gone. "What you got?" says Chris, getting up to look, and he fell over the coffee table, the one where Claire's dad keeps his chess set.

'"Have a whisky," says Claire. At least she'd had the sense not to start drinking before they did. "Look at this, Stu," says Chris. "It's not an ordinary chess set. It's all little people."

'"It's the Isle of Lewis chess set," says Stu. "You know, the one they dug up in the Hebrides that was hundreds of years old."

'"So what's your dad doing with it?" says Chris. "Is it hot? Did he nick it from the British Museum? I never knew your dad was a fence, Hawes."'

'I begin to feel that this Chris is not really our sort of person,' Nazzer said. 'His wit kind of gets you over the back of the neck with a dull thud.'

'Claire was getting really panicky because Chris was shunting the chess men about and her dad's dead fussy about his collectors' items. He orders them from the Sunday supplements and they're all made of resin, but he keeps them locked up in a cabinet. Only he does play chess, it's about the fastest thing he can manage, I think,' Nina said, 'so that's why the set had been left out. Chris was beginning to look mad. He says, "You want a game, Stu?" "Put them down," says Claire. She was getting furious now but Chris says, "I can't. I'm hooked. Aaaaah!" he says, "you should never have let me see them." He was down on his knees and sort of wrestling with a bishop. "I thought I was cured," he says, "but they're right. You're never cured of chess. I gotta play. I gotta play."

'Stu says, "Lay off, Stilwell," but he wouldn't. He was writhing about on the floor with a knight between his teeth. Claire began kicking him but he just kept moaning, "Cold Turkey! I gotta play. Gimme a fix."

'I said, "Haven't you got any ordinary chess men?" and I started collecting up the other pieces before Chris got hold of them. Stu helped. He prised the bishop out of Chris's hand and gave it to me. It was like nicking a dummy off a baby. Chris screams, "You can't do this to me!" and starts clawing at Stu's legs. If he'd clawed *my* leg,' Nina said, 'I'd have booted him in the head, but Stu just said, "Oh, shut up, I'll find you something else to play with. I saw this film once where they played chess with miniatures." "Miniature whats?" says Chris and the knight fell out of his mouth so I grabbed it, quick. "Miniature drink bottles," Stu said, and I saw where he was looking. Mr Hawes keeps this collection of miniatures on the pelmet over the window. "Let's play with those," he says. "Every time you win a piece you have to drink it."

'I said, "They're all empty." I'd have thought Stu would have had more sense.

'"No they're not," says Claire. That's just what I would have expected from her. She climbed on to the settee and started scooping them down – and they *weren't* empty; you could tell by the clunking. She laid them out on the chess board and there weren't nearly enough. "Hang about," says Stu. He took the stuffed olives out of the paté bowl and wiped them, and put *them* out for pawns.

'"What about my prawns?" says Chris. "Pawns," says Stu. "Prunes," says Chris. "That's a thought," says Stu, "you got any prunes?" I thought things were getting a bit out of hand, myself,' Nina said, 'but Claire went stumping off to the kitchen. She'd have brought him pickled onions if he'd asked, she was so relieved *something* was happening. Chris started fossicking in the sideboard and got out the salt and pepper mill and said they'd be *his* king and queen.'

'What about the miniatures?' Maurice said.

'Well,' Nina said, 'that was it. They'd forgotten about them, so when Claire came back with the prunes *I* went out to the kitchen and grabbed everything I could find for rooks and bishops and knights – egg cups, spice jars, almond essence and a salad oil bottle. By the time we'd got that lot out there wasn't space for anything else. We'd got every piece, except for Stu's queen. He was looking round the room for a queen and he suddenly spotted the mermaid. There wasn't really room for her on the square but he squeezed all the other pieces sideways and plonked her down next to the salad oil bottle – that was his king. And the board was ready then. It looked like a fairy banquet – horrible bent fairies who'd been up all night boozing and gambling and smashing windows.'

'If you think about it,' Nazzer said, 'that's very much what fairies must have been like anyway. People seemed to spend most of their time buying them off, like they were running some kind of protection racket. You know the score, a note through the window, wrapped round a brick. *You have been a bit tight with the bread and milk lately, squire. Put one medium sliced and a pint of gold top behind the cistern or the lads will be round to do you over. Signed, Puck.*'

'Stu says, "Your move," and Chris moved one of his prunes. Stu moved an olive. Chris moved another prune and Stu moved an olive and then Chris started going vroom-vroom and zoomed his almond essence out of the back row and took it. And Stu said, "You can't do that with a knight," and Chris says, "It's not a knight, it's a bishop," and eats the olive, quick; and Stu says, "Bishops don't got there," and Chris says, "They do in *my* army." "Right, no holds barred," says Stu, and he got the mermaid by the throat and brought her down on one of the prunes. "Two can play at that game," he says.

'"Now eat it," says Chris. "Not likely," says Stu, and put

the prune to one side, but Chris says, "I ate the olive. It was your idea." "I said we got to drink what we won," says Stu, but Chris said it was the same thing, so Stu ate the prune. Well, he just swallowed it. I don't think he knew that prunes have stones in,' Nina said. 'Anyway, Chris moved his pepper mill and took another olive and then Stu plunged in with the mermaid and captured the almond essence.

'"Now drink that," says Chris. "Get out of it," says Stu, but Chris said, "You won it, you drink it."'

'Stu exhibits a certain lack of foresight, on this showing, don't you think?' Nazzer observed. 'Which amounts almost to imbecility.'

'He kept saying that almond essence was poisonous,' Nina said. 'Actually, he didn't know it *was* almond essence, because it had *Ratafia* on the bottle. I don't think he can ever go into a kitchen. And Claire says, "Go on, Chris, make him drink it," and drapes an arm round his neck like those women in old films who try and get the men to fight and won't have them back until they've been beaten to pulp, but Chris wasn't having any. "That's all I need," he said. "Chess groupies." "Count me out," I said. Chris yells, "Do you think Kasparov became world champion with a woman hanging round his neck?"

'Stu took the lid off the almond essence and swigged. His eyes closed. I didn't even try to guess what it must taste like,' Nina said. 'Cyanide's the nearest, I suppose. Then Chris got his egg cup and took another olive and Stu says, "I've got you sussed, Stilwell. I see why you let me have all the goodies. Every time you take a piece you get a treat. Every time I do I get poisoned." "I'm after your mermaid," says Chris.

'Stu didn't say anything. He went over to the settee and got an armful of cushions, and set them up like sandbags at his end of the table. Then he moved the mermaid behind the sandbags. Chris's eyes got very small. He snaps his fingers at Claire. "Bring me a fork," he says.'

'I must say,' Maurice remarked, 'she does seem to bring out the worst in men. You haven't choked me off yet, you know.'

'You don't have to *bring* out the worst in Chris,' Nina said. 'It oozes out through his pores. I thought Chris wanted the fork to go after the mermaid with, but he laid the tines on the table, put a prune on the handle and twanged it. And the prune shot up in the air, over the sandbags.

"Right," says Stu, "say your prayers, Stilwell," and he went over to the fireplace and fetched the poker.'

'I thought it was an electric fire,' Maurice said.

'It is,' Nina said, 'but they've got a poker and a shovel and a hearth brush all hung up from a stand, and this fancy coal bucket made of brass with a galleon on the side. Stu stood with his feet apart at his end of the table and swung the poker a few times and teed-off with an olive.

'"Put that down!" says Claire. She was crawling about on the floor, looking for prunes, because Chris was firing at will. And Stu started yelling, "Now Stu Ballesteros will go for a hole in one!" and took another swing and hit the pepper mill. Chris goes, "Now eat that," but of course Stu wouldn't . . .'

'Why of course?' Nazzer inquired.

'. . . So Chris got the pepper mill and started grinding it over Stu's head.'

'You mentioned cannibals, earlier,' Nazzer said. 'Can we look forward to seeing Stu *eaten* in the next reel?'

'Stu rolled across the floor and stuck his head in the coal bucket – for safe keeping. When he stood up again he was wearing it. It came right down over his neck. Chris hit him over the head with the hearth brush and he sort of clanged and Stu was laying about with the poker and not hitting Chris because he couldn't see where he was going. Then he started doing robotic movements, all stiff and slow. "I am an android," he says. "I am Zenner Diode, curse of the great black hole in Orion. I am programmed to destroy the galaxy – starting with Stilwell."'

'That's quite good, really,' Maurice conceded. 'I like that – Zenner Diode. Is he into electronics?'

'What's electronics got to do with it?' Nina said. 'He fell over one of the coffee tables and Chris jumped on him. "I am Luke Skyscraper," he says. "I am going to zap you, Zenner Diode." Claire was still crawling about looking for prunes. She was really in a snot, now. "I thought you were supposed to be playing *chess*," she says, and Stu goes, "This is Galactic Chess," and Chris goes, "Kamikaze Chess!" and spread his arms and dived on Stu and they both hit the floor with this terrible clang from the coal bucket. Claire lost her rag and grabbed the poker and started whanging the coal bucket and screaming "Get up! Get out!" We didn't hear the door open.

'None of us noticed anything,' Nina said, 'until this voice comes out of the coal bucket: "I can see four little feet, all in a row," and we looked round and saw the feet, and the legs, and Mr and Mrs Hawes standing in the doorway. Claire stood up. Her eyes went all swively and frightened. I was glad she had the poker and not me because the coal bucket was all over dents. Chris came out from behind the cushions and Stu climbed out of the coal bucket. Mrs Hawes said, "You're drunk."

'Claire started to say no, but her dad sort of turned on her and she shut up. "You've been drinking," says Mrs Hawes, and this time Chris said no but he started hiccuping – from shock probably. That didn't help. It came out no-ho-ho-ho-ho.

'"You have," says Claire's dad and she said, "We haven't. Look at the bottles. They haven't been opened. Even the open ones aren't open."

'"You've had something," says her mum, and Stu says, "Ratafia," and you could smell it. You could smell something else, too, but we didn't know what it was. Mr and Mrs Hawes noticed, because they started sniffing. I know what *they* thought it was, though. They'd heard about young tearaways and drink-and-drugs parties, you could tell. Old man Hawes is a PE teacher. *He* knows how to deal with young tearaways. "You've been taking – *things*," he says, like he knew all about it so there was no point in us arguing. "Substances," he says. "Where do you get them? Who supplies you?" Stu woke up then, when Mr Hawes said supplies. He suddenly realized what Hawes was on about. "You mean you think we're stoned?" he says. "I mean," says Hawes, "if you haven't been drinking you must have been taking something. What was it?" Chris just goes "U-hurk!" but Stu was furious. He said, "We haven't been taking anything." "Don't lie to me, boy," says Hawes, and you could just imagine him in the gym, being God in a track suit. "How else did you get into this state?" And we all looked round, then. You could see what he meant. There were cushions all over the place and scarves, and the carpet was covered with prunes and olives and egg cups, and the mermaid was leaking all over the rug, and there was this *smell*, almonds and something else, that Claire's mum and dad thought was pot or heroin. Stu sort of mumbled, "I dunno. Must have been adrenalin or something." Nobody said anything. I mean, the room looked like elephants had been *raped* in it. No way could you blame that on adrenalin. But Claire thought her mum and dad didn't know what Stu was talking about, though there must be plenty of adrenalin in PE. She says, "It's an enzyme."

'They didn't believe her. Mrs Hawes started crying and Mr Hawes clouted Claire and Claire started crying. Chris and Stu were offering to clear up but I thought it would be better if they just went, so I saw them out. They seemed to sober up on the doorstep. I suppose it was the fresh air,' Nina said, 'only of course, they *were* sober. Mind you,' said Nina, 'I'd hate to meet them if they really were stoned.'

'It's a hormone,' Maurice said.

'What?'

'Adrenalin's a hormone. Produced by the adrenal gland, downwind of the kidneys.'

'My god,' Nina said, 'it's a good thing Claire got that

wrong. If her mum and dad had known there were hormones involved they'd have called the Vice Squad in. That funny smell, though – it was the mermaid. I'm glad they never tried drinking her; she was full of aftershave.'

'I think innocence in adults is terrifying,' Nazzer said.

MEN ONLY

———————— ◆ ————————

Those creatures with two legs and eight hands.
Jayne Mansfield

IF MEN COULD MENSTRUATE

◆

Gloria Steinem

A white minority of the world has spent centuries conning us into thinking that a white skin makes people superior – even though the only thing it really does is make them more subject to ultraviolet rays and to wrinkles. Male human beings have built whole cultures around the idea that penis-envy is 'natural' to women – though having such an un-protected organ might be said to make men vulnerable, and the power to give birth makes womb-envy at least as logical.

In short, the characteristics of the powerful, whatever they may be, are thought to be better than the characteristics of the powerless – and logic has nothing to do with it.

What would happen, for instance, if suddenly, magically, men could menstruate and women could not?

The answer is clear – menstruation would become an envi-able, boast-worthy, masculine event:

Men would brag about how long and how much.

Boys would mark the onset of menses, that longed-for proof of manhood, with religious ritual and stag parties.

Congress would fund a National Institute of Dysmenor-rhea to help stamp out monthly discomforts.

Sanitary supplies would be federally funded and free. (Of course, some men would still pay for the prestige of commer-cial brands such as John Wayne Tampons, Muhammad Ali's Rope-a-dope Pads, Joe Namath's Jock Shields – 'For Those

Light Bachelor Days,' and Robert 'Baretta' Blake Maxi-Pads.)

Military men, right-wing politicians, and religious fundamentalists would cite menstruation ('*men*-struation') as proof that only men could serve in the Army ('you have to give blood to take blood'), occupy political office ('can women be aggressive without that steadfast cycle governed by the planet Mars?'), be priests and ministers ('how could a woman give her blood for our sins?'), or rabbis ('without the monthly loss of impurities, women remain unclean').

Male radicals, left-wing politicians, and mystics, however, would insist that women are equal, just different, and that any woman could enter their ranks if only she were willing to self-inflict a major wound every month ('you *must* give blood for the revolution'), recognize the preeminence of menstrual issues, or subordinate her selfness to all men in their Cycle of Enlightenment.

Street guys would brag ('I'm a three-pad man') or answer praise from a buddy ('Man, you lookin' *good!*') by giving fives and saying, 'Yeah, man, I'm on the rag!'

TV shows would treat the subject at length. (*Happy Days*: Richie and Potsie try to convince Fonzie that he is still 'The Fonz,' though he has missed two periods in a row.) So would newspapers. (SHARK SCARE THREATENS MENSTRUATING MEN. JUDGE CITES MONTHLY STRESS IN PARDONING RAPIST.) And movies. (Newman and Redford in *Blood Brothers*!)

Men would convince women that intercourse was *more* pleasurable at 'that time of the month.' Lesbians would be said to fear blood and therefore life itself – though probably only because they needed a good menstruating man.

Of course, male intellectuals would offer the most moral and logical arguments. How could a woman master any discipline that demanded a sense of time, space, mathematics, or measurement, for instance, without that in-built gift for measuring the cycles of the moon and planets – and thus for measuring anything at all? In the rarefied fields of philosophy and religion, could women compensate for missing the rhythm of the universe? Or for their lack of symbolic death-and-resurrection every month?

Liberal males in every field would try to be kind: the fact that 'these people' have no gift for measuring life or connecting to the universe, the liberals would explain, should be punishment enough.

And how would women be trained to react? One can imagine traditional women agreeing to all these arguments with a staunch and smiling masochism. ('The ERA would force housewives to wound themselves every month': Phyllis Schlafly. 'Your husband's blood is as sacred as that of Jesus – and so sexy, too!': Marabel Morgan.) Reformers and Queen Bees would try to imitate men, and *pretend* to have a monthly cycle. All feminists would explain endlessly that men, too, needed to be liberated from the false idea of Martian aggressiveness, just as women needed to escape the bonds of menses-envy. Radical feminists would add that the oppression of the nonmenstrual was the pattern for all other oppressions. ('Vampires were our first freedom fighters!') Cultural feminists would develop a bloodless imagery in art and literature. Socialist feminists would insist that only under capitalism would men be able to monopolize menstrual blood.

In fact, if men could menstruate, the power justifications would probably go on forever.

If we let them.

MY LOVER

◆

Wendy Cope

For I will consider my lover, who shall remain
nameless.
For at the age of 49 he can make the noise of five
different kinds of lorry changing gear on a hill.
For he sometimes does this on the stairs at his place of
work.
For he is embarrassed when people overhear him.
For he can also imitate at least three different kinds of
train.
For these include the London tube train, the steam
engine, and the Southern Rail electric.
For he supports Tottenham Hotspur with joyful and
unswerving devotion.
For he abhors Arsenal, whose supporters are
uncivilized and rough.
For he explains that Spurs are magic, whereas Arsenal
are boring and defensive.
For I knew nothing of this six months ago, nor did I
want to.
For now it all enchants me.
For this he performs in ten degrees.
For first he presents himself as a nice, serious, liberated
person.
For secondly he sits through many lunches, discussing
life and love and never mentioning football.

For thirdly he is careful not to reveal how much he
   dislikes losing an argument.

For fourthly he talks about the women in his past,
   acknowledging that some of it must have been his
   fault.

For fifthly he is so obviously reasonable that you are
   inclined to doubt this.

For sixthly he invites himself round for a drink one
   evening.

For seventhly you consume two bottles of wine between
   you.

For eighthly he stays the night.

For ninthly you cannot wait to see him again.

For tenthly he does not get in touch for several days.

For having achieved his object he turns again to his
   other interests.

For he will not miss his evening class or his choir
   practice for a woman.

For he is out nearly all the time.

For you cannot even get him on the telephone.

For he is the kind of man who has been driving women
   round the bend for generations.

For, sad to say, this thought does not bring you to your
   senses.

For he is charming.

For he is good with animals and children.

For his voice is both reassuring and sexy.

For he drives an A-registration Vauxhall Astra estate.

For he goes at 80 miles per hour on the motorways.

For when I plead with him he says, 'I'm not going any
   slower than *this*.'

For he is convinced he knows his way around better
   than anyone else on earth.

For he does not encourage suggestions from his
   passengers.

For if he ever got lost there would be hell to pay.

For he sometimes makes me sleep on the wrong side of
  my own bed.

For he cannot be bossed around.

For he has this grace, that he is happy to eat fish fingers
  or Chinese takeaway or to cook the supper himself.

For he knows about my cooking and is realistic.

For he makes me smooth cocoa with bubbles on the top.

For he drinks and smokes at least as much as I do.

For he is obsessed with sex.

For he would never say it is overrated.

For he grew up before the permissive society and
  remembers his adolescence.

For he does not insist it is healthy and natural, nor does
  he ask me what I would like him to do.

For he has a few ideas of his own.

For he has never been able to sleep much and talks with
  me late into the night.

For we wear each other out with our wakefulness.

For he makes me feel like a light-bulb that cannot switch
  itself off.

For he inspires poem after poem.

For he is clean and tidy but not too concerned with his
  appearance.

For he lets the barber cut his hair too short and goes
  round looking like a convict for a fortnight.

For when I ask if this necklace is all right he replies,
  'Yes, if no means looking at three others.'

For he was shocked when younger team-mates began
  using talcum powder in the changing-room.

For his old-fashioned masculinity is the cause of
  continual merriment on my part.

For this puzzles him.

NICE MEN

◆

Dorothy Byrne

I know a nice man who is kind to his wife
and always lets her do what she wants.

I heard of another nice man who killed his
girlfriend. It was an accident. He pushed her
in a quarrel and she split open her skull on the
dining-room table. He was such a guilt-ridden
sight in court that the jury felt sorry for him.

My friend Aiden is nice. He thinks women are
really equal.

There are lots of nice men who help their wives
with the shopping and the housework.

And many men, when you are alone with
them, say, 'I prefer women. They are so
understanding.' This is another example of
men being nice.

Some men, when you make a mistake at work,
just laugh. They don't go on about it or shout.
That's nice.

At times, the most surprising men will say at
parties, 'There's a lot to this Women's Lib.'
Here again, is a case of men behaving in a nice
way.

Another nice thing is that some men are
sympathetic when their wives feel unhappy.
I've often heard men say, 'Don't worry about
everything so much, dear.'

You hear stories of men who are far more than
nice – putting women in lifeboats first, etc.

Sometimes when a man has not been nice, he
apologises and trusts you with intimate details
of the pressures in his life. This just shows how
nice he is, underneath.

I think that is all I can say on the subject of
nice men. Thank you.

PENIS-ENVY

♦

Fiona Pitt-Kethley

Freud, you were right! I must expose my id
And show the penis-envy that lies hid.
It's not that I admire the look as such,
It seems a strange adornment for a crutch,
Like sets of giblets from a butcher's shop,
Two kidneys with a chicken-neck on top,
Floating serene in baths like lug-worm bait,
Or, jokily bobbing with the jogger's gait.
Fig-leaves, I'm sure, are prettier far than cocks,
And only suffer greenfly not the pox.
As tools, pricks really aren't reliable,
One minute hard, the next too pliable.
If I had bought a hammer or a chisel
As changeable, I'd think it was a swizzle.

It's not that I'm against them in their place,
But simply that I cannot see a case
For cocks to be a sort of union card
In life's closed shop. I think it very hard
That humans with these fickle bits and bobs
Are given a fairer lot and better jobs.
If only I'd had one of them, it seems
I could have had success, fulfilled my dreams.
A female eunuch though, all I'll attain
Is Pyrrhic victory and trifling gain.

How to Get a Man (I'm Serious)

Cynthia Heimel

♦

I know what men want.
    Men want a lady in the living room and a whore in the bedroom.

Men want women's hair to be fragrant and shiny and long. Long hair is feminine.

Men want women to be feminine.

The way to a man's heart is through his stomach.

Men want a gourmet cook. Men want a woman who can serve a four-course meal at a moment's notice.

Men want a woman with a sense of humor.

Men want to be mothered.

Men want smooth, firm buttocks.

Men don't like a hard, competitive, tough woman. She makes men feel threatened. If they feel threatened in one regard, they feel threatened in all regards. This way lies impotence.

Men don't want a doormat. If they can walk all over you, they won't respect you. If you want a man to marry you, be a demanding bitch.

Men want a certain air of mystery. Don't tell him where you're going, what you're doing. Smile enigmatically. Keep secrets. Have flowers with suggestive notes attached delivered to yourself and blush with confusion when he notices them.

Men want a nice set of knockers.

Men want an athletic woman, an outdoorsy woman, a woman who is in fine, muscular shape. A woman with a decent tennis serve.

Men want women who will share their interests and hobbies.

Men want a good pair of legs.

Men want well-groomed women with clean, shapely fingernails and a dainty scent.

Men want women to wear high heels so that their ass projects outward.

A man wants a woman who will understand him. A woman who knows why he gets melancholy on Sunday afternoons.

A man wants a woman with a small, trim waist.

A man wants a helpmeet.

A man wants a slut. He wants a woman who will be a tiger in bed, a woman who has a huge sexual appetite and massive erotic skill. A man wants a tireless, inventive sex-slave.

A man can't stand even a hint of desperation.

A man will want you much more when he thinks he can't have you. The way to get a man is to come on strong and then run away.

A man wants a woman he can show off to his friends.

A man wants a woman who can hold her liquor.

'Oh, blow me,' says this man who was in my bed a minute ago and is now reading over my shoulder.

'Nice talk,' I say, 'very nice.'

'How dare you decide what *men* want? As if all men were the same. Don't you realize how demeaning that is?'

'I know, don't you think I know? I'm just trying to whip the reader into a frenzy of rebellion! I'm bludgeoning her with the conventional wisdom! I don't mean a word of it, okay?'

'Blow me anyway,' he says, climbing back into bed.

The thing is, when women get lonely and scared we *believe things*.

Say it's raining outside, you're coming home from your boring office-temp job, you throw open the door to your apartment and collapse into a frenzy of tears.

You just can't bear the idea of spending one more hideous evening on your sofa, staring at your same old knickknacks, misting your goddamned philodendron, popping another stupid Lean Cuisine in the microwave, and sniffling over another episode of *Murphy Brown*. You need a life. You need a man. Or you'll grow crazy.

You call your Aunt Susan. She tells you to buy a garter belt and seamed stockings and wear red lipstick.

You read a magazine which tells you to match your body language to his, and to use positive imaging. You practise picturing every aspect of the man of your dreams so that he will ring your doorbell, preferably within ten seconds.

You read a self-help book which gives you a fifteen-step program at the end of which you're supposed to realize that wanting a man is just an addiction and a stupid addiction at that.

Your head swims with man-getting information. Your brain is jangled with advice and instructions that you get dizzy and have to put your head between your legs.

What to do?

Okay, pay attention now: I have the ultimate man-getting advice. You don't have to listen to anybody else. Just listen to me. Okay, here's what you do:

Nothing.

If he's the wrong man, you can turn yourself inside out with wiles and perfume and French maid's outfits and nothing will work. You'll never get him, you'll never keep him, you don't have a chance.

If he's the right man, you can have greasy hair, spinach in your teeth, and your skirt on inside out, and he'll still be entranced and follow you to the ends of the earth.

You don't have to believe me, but what I say is absolutely true. You just have to follow your own personal, weird, goofy little star and some poor sucker is going to come along and die for you.

Let me tell you about Nora, who was heartbroken. She hadn't had a real boyfriend in about ten years, and the man she had been dating and crazy about had just vanished. She was depressed, discouraged, devastated. She couldn't understand why men never noticed her.

'Maybe it's the way you dress,' I said.

'What's wrong with the way I dress?' she asked.

'Well, like right now you look like you're wearing a series of lampshades. Is there a body under there?'

'This is the way we dressed in Kansas.'

'We're not in Kansas anymore, Toto. Buy a miniskirt. Show some cleavage. Men like that.'

Stubborn girl wouldn't listen. Soon she didn't have to. Mr Perfect reappeared. 'I miss you,' he told her. 'I miss those ratbag outfits of yours.' That was a year ago. They are now discussing marriage.

Everybody's different. Some men (okay, only a few) hate garter belts. Some hate all makeup and adore enormous, clunky shoes. Some men wouldn't even look at Michelle Pfeiffer if she appeared at their door in a negligee and begged for it. Men, yes even men, are human. And you can't second-guess a human being. Try and make a science of romance one minute, the next minute you're checking into a loony bin.

That man over there in my bed? I used to doll myself up. One Tuesday morning I went to the post office in ratty sweats, zero makeup, and my hair a frazzle. There he was.

'Don't look at me!' I shrieked, hiding behind the wanted posters.

He looked at me. 'You looked really adorable,' he said, and kissed me. His eyes shone so I knew he meant it.

Okay, the second part of my advice is just as simple but infinitely harder:

To get a man, you have to be ready for a man.

Taking a man into your life is an enormous risk. Can you

open your heart to a man, can you be trusting and vulnerable knowing that you're also opening yourself up to the possibility of rejection and heartbreak? Can you withstand rejection and heartbreak? Can you let another person inside your defenses, let him know who you really are and what you're really like, knowing that he might someday leave you? Can you bear it?

No, neither can I. But I'm trying. It's quite a trick to build up your defenses against heartbreak and yet not be defensive against men. And the trick is to develop self-confidence. Which is quite a trick, especially when you're feeling needy and desperate.

But be brave. Have a good look at yourself. Are you torturing yourself for your singleness? Punishing yourself for your alleged failure? Eating hundreds of thousands of M&Ms to atone for your neediness and desperation?

Our society has made a practice of punishing its victims. Not only are women being punished (still!) for the feminist movement, but, even worse, they are being flayed alive for feeling weak and dependent and in need of love. Society has taught women to hate themselves.

Society sucks. Pay it no mind. Of course you feel lonely and desperate and want love! You're human! Wanting love is an honourable wish!

When you stop practising self-hatred, when you start feeling affection for yourself and your little ways, when you are able to follow that weird and goofy little star of yours, then your fears and defenses fall from you like thistledown. Then you're ready for a man.

And then the nightmare begins.

MY LIFE AS A MAN

◆

Alice Kahn

I can't make it in this man's world. Life would be so much easier if I had a wife. Life would be so much easier if I were a man.

What modern woman hasn't had these thoughts? Those of us struggling to lift ourselves up by our bra straps often feel the deck is stacked against us. Men don't have to 'prove' anything. Men can do an OK job; women have to be great. Men were taught from childhood to be aggressive; we were taught to be nice. Men are encouraged to go for it; we are encouraged to lose weight.

In an attempt to understand what the world looks like to someone who has all these advantages, I decided to be Man for a Day. What would happen, I wondered, if I walked a mile in his big leather shoes? A bit of makeup, a few new items of clothing, a different haircut and – *voilà* – little Alice became Big Al.

The first thing I noticed was the frightened look on my husband's face when he woke up and saw me standing there dousing myself with Stud, the aftershave for men who want to make a stink.

I was about to say, 'You get those buns out of bed and make me some breakfast' when I realized that I hadn't made him breakfast since our fifth anniversary. Sure, for a few years I

142

cooked, cleaned and was his all-around love slave. But after a while it was every person for itself.

Later, one of the kids took a look at me in my baggy pleated pants, felt hat, suspenders and tie and said, 'Mom, don't try to be cool. Maybe Diane Keaton can get away with that, but it just isn't you.'

As soon as they were all out of the house, instead of my usual routine of not cleaning up and not doing the laundry, I put on my moustache and went out.

As I walked down the street I heard a man who passed me say, 'Who was that? Madonna?'

'You've been listening to Joan Rivers,' said his companion. 'That was Wayne Newton.'

I could pass.

At the office, I introduced myself to the guys as Big Al, the new guy.

'Hey, Big Al the New Guy,' one of the fellas said, 'want to go deer hunting with us after work? We're gonna kill for a couple of hours, then pick up some babes and party.'

'Sorry,' I said. 'Can't make it.'

'Whatsa matter, Al – you a sissy-boy?'

As if that weren't enough, the boss called me in at nine-fifteen. 'Scotch, Al?' he said, offering me the bottle from the brown paper bag on his desk.

I declined. 'Whatsa matter, Al – can't handle it?'

At lunchtime, I went to my favorite bar and grill. Instead of getting the Dieter's Delight, I told the waitress: 'Give me the biggest, bloodiest, rawest hunk of meat you've got, a plate of fries, double coleslaw and some chocolate whipped-cream pie.'

'No wonder you're so thin,' she said. 'You eat like a bird.'

After lunch I walked over to the bookstore, hoping to find something hard-boiled to carry around but not actually read.

'Where's the Men's section?' I asked the clerk.

'We have no Men's section,' she answered.

'But that's not fair,' I said indignantly. 'You have a Women's section.'

'Look, pal,' she said to me, her voice dripping with sarcasm, 'we consider the rest of the store the Men's section.'

Back at work, I noticed Marge, the gofer, staring at me. I stared back at her. I was certain she'd guessed my identity.

'Marge, guess what's under here?' I said, smiling at her.

She stood up on her desk and started screaming, 'Eek, a pervert!'

My sexual-harassment hearing is scheduled for next week.

When the boss heard about the charges, he offered me a raise. And the guys are taking me out to dinner. Phyllis, a gal in the secretarial pool, winked at me and said she would testify on my behalf. Then she asked if I would take her to the annual spring dance.

I think I'll wear a tux.

Just a Housewife?

♦

I hate housework. You make the beds, you wash the dishes –
and six months later you have to start all over again.
Joan Rivers

Why did I never marry? Just lucky, I guess.
Gloria Steinem

Had we but world enough and time,
This note would be a Valentine.
Since married life is what we have,
It's just to remind you to bring home the
haddock and the Sanilav
Libby Purves

Sluts – I

◆

Katharine Whitehorn

This article is dedicated to all those who have ever changed their stockings in a taxi, brushed their hair with someone else's nailbrush or safety-pinned a hem; and those who have not had probably better not read on.

Anyone in doubt, however, can ask herself the following questions. Have you ever taken anything back out of the dirty-clothes basket because it had become, relatively, the cleaner thing? How many things are there, at this moment, in the wrong room – cups in the study, boots in the kitchen; and how many of them are on the *floor* of the wrong room?

Could you try on clothes in any shop, any time, without worrying about your underclothes? And how, if at all, do you clean your nails? Honest answers should tell you, once and for all, whether you are one of us: the miserable, optimistic, misunderstood race of sluts.

We are not ordinary human beings who have degenerated, as people think: we are born this way. Even at four you can pick us out: the little girls in the playground who have one pant-leg hanging down and no hair-slide; at ten we are the ones who look dirty even when we are clean (unlike the goodigoodies who look unfairly clean when they are dirty); and at fifteen, when black stockings are fashionable, we be-tray ourselves in the changing-room by legs spotted like a

Dalmatian's, the inevitable result of using Indian ink instead of darning-wool.

People who are not sluts intolerantly assume that we must like things this way, without realizing the enormous effort and inconvenience that goes into being so ineffective: the number of times we have to fill the car's radiator because we don't get it mended, the fortunes we spend on taxis going back for parcels we have left in shops, the amount of ironing occasioned by our practice of unpacking not so much when we get back from a week-end as four days later.

We acquire, it is true, certain off-beat skills: I am much better at holding a bottle of varnish between two fingers than those of my friends who do not paint their nails in the Tube, and they cannot cut their nails with a pen-knife, either; but nothing really makes up to us for the difficulties of our way of life.

However, I am not trying to make a soggy bid for sympathy so much as to work out what we can possibly do to improve our condition. And the first thing, it seems to me, is to inscribe *Abandon Hope All Ye Who Enter Here* over the lintels of all our messy houses; for it is our optimism that is principally our undoing. We keep hoping that we will remember to wash our white collars, or find time to comb our hair on the way to the office, or slide into the building and dump our coats before anyone can see that there are three buttons missing. More, it seems to me, could be done if we could only face up realistically to all the things we never will be able to do.

We can realize, for example, that no power on earth is going to make us look well turned out all, or even most, of the time. We can therefore give up right away any New Year resolutions about fashion: a second pair of little white gloves will simply result in our carrying two right hands; wigs would be a waste of money because those of us who cannot keep our real hair tidy cannot keep our toy hair tidy either. Instead, we can wear reasonably sober clothes normally, go for stacked heels because we know we won't remember to get them reheeled before they are worn down, have only one colour of accessories, so that we cannot wear the brown shoes with the black bag.

And, having accepted that people are *not* going to say 'she's always so chic', we can concentrate every now and then on really dazzling efforts that will knock our audience sideways. Jane Austen was right when she said that no beauty accustomed to compliments ever got anything like the thrill of an ordinary looker who was told she was looking terrific *that evening*.

We can give up making good resolutions about replacing things before they run out, which is absurd, and concentrate instead on bulk buying, so that the gap between supply and supply happens much more rarely. We can also, of course, keep icing sugar, the wrong sort of rice, tea bags, a spearmint toothpaste and so on specifically to tide us over when we do run out of the real thing. It is true that we tend not to have any money either, but as we usually spend what we have at the beginning of the month like drunken sailors anyway, we might as well spend it on vast tubs of cleansing cream, acres of Kleenex (which we have to have, since clean handkerchiefs, let's face it, are beyond us), sugar in ten-pound bags.

Apart from this sort of grim realism, there are, I think, only two other things that can help us. The first is habit: odd as it may seem, even sluts do occasionally acquire good habits (we clean our teeth, for example, even if we sometimes have to do it with soap) and these, indeed, are all that hold us together. A slut who baths whenever she has time never baths at all: her only hope is to get up into one every morning; if she shops here and there for food there will never be any around, but a Saturday supermarket raid will settle a whole week's hash at one go.

And the second is money: for the only way a slut can really get things done is to get someone else to do them. Even the most domestic slut will find it worth earning a few pounds to pay for help in the house.

The only way to make up for missing the post is a long-distance telephone call; the only way not to have to go back to fetch things is to get them picked up by messenger. The only thing that will get a slut's carpets vacuumed daily is a daily. All sluts ought to be, or to marry, rich people: and I treasure the hope that among the really rich there may be dozens of sluts lurking undetected by the rest.

Money, low cunning and a sense of realism may help us somewhat; but it is a hard life all the same. I wrote this article two years ago, but as it was felt that it hardly came well from the pen of a fashion editor, it was never printed. So I thought I had a soft option using it now; except that, of course, I couldn't find it, and have had to write the whole blasted thing again.

SLUTS – II

A couple of months ago I owned up in this column to being a slut. It was absolutely splendid: I found that there were scores of us, all struggling away.

There was the woman who had got to be a dab hand at identifying lettuce in the dark, as she never remembered to pick it by daylight; and the one who said she couldn't have a daily help – it was too much effort clearing up before she came. There was one who cited her six children as proof of her sluthood, in one direction at least; and the mother who claimed that (thanks to a scarf in the wrong washing-machine load) her baby was the only one in Ruislip with blue nappies.

Men, too – they call it 'slob': one wrote in block capitals by candlelight having run out of shillings for the meter, and another said he stapled his braces to his trousers when all buttons failed.

Some sluts had come to terms with their state: 'We now live on a small yacht; it solves a lot of problems' – presumably much of the mess simply falls over the side and is washed away. Others were still protesting: '*Why* are there no three-way mirrors even in first-class carriages?' A good many offered suggestions on thwarting the second law of thermo-dynamics which is the tendency of everything in the universe towards dissolution and decay.

Their suggestions were colourful to the point of being lurid. There was this business of keeping suspenders going when the bobble is off: many rejected aspirins, on the ground that sluts never have any (but use gin for headaches instead), and instead advocated corn rings and coins; one said, 'I used the buttons off my husband's pyjamas till he sewed them on again.'

Shoulder straps can be kept going with a paperclip, and one woman even suggested that if both straps have gone you can keep a slip up by wearing your bra outside it. (To my mind, one should go in for vests and slips that are strapless on purpose, I mean made that way, and stay up accordingly.)

Plainly, sluts should not wear seamed nylons, as it is the seams that usually betray the fact that the stockings are not a pair – and ladders show less in pale than in patterned stock-ings. Sluts should get all necessary hems shortened at the time of purchase, since they will never actually get around to doing it themselves; and, apropos of hems, they should keep a ready supply of black safety pins.

Many would agree that colourless pearl nail varnish shows

chips less than coloured – but if the varnish is to hide London grime as well, three coats per nail is a minimum. For any dress that has a little white collar, a slut should also buy some white beads, for the collar's off-days; and all sluts should have bathroom curtains made of towelling for the times when the guest is in the bathroom but the towels are in the hot-cupboard.

Sluts have special problems in the kitchen. Any slut must at all costs avoid a pressure cooker, or sooner or later she will leave it too long (like all those other blackened pans) and blow herself up. She needs a lot of Kleenex, both for sitting a cup on when the saucer is sloppy, and for wiping round a pan out of which fat has spilled: if you don't, as I know from bitter experience, the fat down the side of the pan acts as a fuse to the gas and the whole thing goes up in a sheet of flame.

One slut asserts sadly that 'you cannot make white sauce with custard powder'; another recommends double sinks – so that when one is stacked with dirty crocks you can still wash the cup you need in the other. I myself am a great believer in wooden plates since you cannot break them; though I have to admit that you can – I have – set them on fire.

When it comes to entertaining, sluts should beware the *second* time. The first time you cook anything, you go care-fully and may get it right; the second, the chances are you think you remember it better than you do or overcorrect on small faults; and disaster follows.

No slut could be expected to keep a hostess book, but one book which is useful is a book like an address-book as a check on all other cookery books: you look up veal, say, and it gives you your six different recipes with the books they come in and page numbers. This begins by being exactly the sort of pointless time-consuming piece of reorganization that sluts love, and ends by being an effective way of stopping you either cooking the same thing over and over, or embarking on the right dish but the wrong recipe.

Sluts should buy stamped envelopes, as half of them never

have stamps and the other half never have envelopes; they should go in for string bags because their overloaded paper carriers always burst.

Those who have desks can stratify the mess on them by putting a layer of newspaper over it all and starting again – the dates on the newspapers then tell the slut what the paleolithic shells tell the geologist (though one don in Cambridge who does this is said to have buried his umbrella on his desk – open).

One could go on forever. No one was able to suggest a way in which sluts could cure themselves of the disease known in my home town as 'doing a Whitehorn' – taking endless trouble to save yourself trouble, so that you clean an oil-lamp rather than walk to the corner of the road to buy a new bulb, or throw cushions at a door for ten minutes rather than get up and shut it.

The only serious spur to tidying up is generally agreed to be visitors – the only drawback being that after they have gone your Pelmanism has to be even better than usual if you are ever to find anything again. But sluts are good at using memory as a substitute for tidiness – though I absolutely deny that I ever said (as friends allege): 'If you're looking for the tax forms they're under your slippers in the salad-bowl.'

HOUSEHOLD HINTS

♦

Phyllis Diller

I'm very good at household hints. I'll give you an example. Supposing you are a housewife and you have goofed. Well, let's put it this way – it's 4:30 and you're still in bed. And you know, that's gettin' pretty close to overtime. And when the beast comes home, the beauty better be ready. So here's the way you play that. You put a little O'Cedar wax behind each ear. It makes you smell tired. It works ... and I've developed something to with leftover sauerkraut. See, you can only do it in December, though. Silver it and hang it on the tree. It stinks but it's beautiful. You see, I consider this creative home-making when things happen and you take it ... well, all right, our stove broke down one day – I mean way down – well, to the basement. Well, there was something heavy in it ... a cupcake. So I tell you what I did. I heated his dinner in the dryer. And I admit it was a mess. But it was hot. So I realized that I would have to treat him rather graciously which was gonna be pretty unnatural – at that time of day. So I read a couple of chapters of *Peyton Place* and a little Norman Vincent Peale. And I even put on a dress ... over my bluejeans. And when I say I kissed him – he thought he was in the wrong house. Until one of the kids bit him. The way we know they're growing up, the bite marks are higher. So I brought him in the house, I sat him down, I put this food in front of him and right away he starts with the beef – he says, 'Okay, what is this stuff on top? You know I hate coconut.' I said, 'Eat it, it's lint.' How did I know he had given up lint for Lent?

DULCIE DOMUM'S BAD HOUSEKEEPING

(AN EXTRACT)

◆

Sue Limb

Obliging young plumber has gone. At his magic touch the bidet has awoken from its sleep of ages and now flushes hot and cold, as indeed do I, in memory of his visit. Tom. Perfect Old English name. Lovely springy curls (could not help noticing as he grovelled at my feet, fiddling with the lucky old copper piping). Admired my children's books, which he reads to his nephew. Also liked my Portuguese tile – something nobody else has ever even noticed.

Sacra conversazione in bathroom interrupted by Henry who burst in yelling, 'I want a poo now quick! It's looking out of my bottom!'

Reluctant goodbye on doorstep. Tom offers to come round immediately if ever I have any trouble, but fear it would only lead to worse trouble still. Besides, no prospect of burst pipe for months; perhaps, with Greenhouse Effect, never again.

Furtively kick radiators hoping to dislodge something vital, and encourage children to thrust Play-Doh down the plugholes, but in vain. Plumbing functions serenely for the first time ever.

Spouse snorts contemptuously at Tom's Anarchist/Buddhist Plumbing Collective bill. 'I see the Buddhism is extra,' he observes acidly. Wonder if this is Spouse's habitual misanthropy or something more interesting.

Listen to Schubert's *String Quartet*. Tears of vague longing pour down cheeks. Henry comes in and says: 'Switch off that stupid music, Mummy, I want Roland Rat.'

Feel Henry is becoming a barbarian. Can see him heading straight for *Vorsprung Durch Technik*. As for Harriet: my entire educational strategy has collapsed. Maternal insistence on Girls are Best, plus relentless exposure to 100% hand-crafted traditional fairy tales, has given her Princess complex. Yearns for silky hair a yard long, bri-nylon tutu and kitsch Prince in lurex tights.

Have definitely failed as Mother, Wife, and Gardener. (Seed potatoes still shrivelling patiently in their string bag.) Also as best-selling writer. Publisher's advance long gone. Warned Spouse about this yesterday and he made dark noises about my having to take on a bit of A-level coaching again. Wonder if Tom the Plumber has, or would like, A-level Eng. Lit. Probably has it already, but could do different Board.

Mind you, literature dangerous thing. Attribute all my problems to having been presented with *Madame Bovary, Le Rouge et le Noir*, and *Anna Karenina* in first term at Newnham. Conclusion: only possible destinies for married woman: adultery or drudgery. Have failed as drudge too: once more cupboard is bare. Put on extremely ancient lentils to boil.

Sound of letters cascading into hall reminds me that I have also failed *vis-à-vis* the Inland Revenue, Electricity Board, etc. Observe large spiders' webs festooning front door. Perhaps could get house designated Nature Reserve.

Distracted by phone. Mysterious Sally. Declares she was devastated to find me absent in Paris when she came to work with Spouse on index for their book. Hopes I was having a Naughty Time. Silly cow. Wonder if this is because she was also having Naughty Time. Think perhaps not. Suspect Spouse on the whole too lazy for adulterous passion. Sally insists we dine with them in Dulwich when next in town. Promise listlessly to do so, curiously aware that somehow have become bored with Sally.

Notice postcard lying on floor with other post. Beautiful italic handwriting. Unfamiliar. Try to read signature upside down: MOT? Wait! ... Tom! Vital organs convulsed with strange and silly spasm. Seize card with trembling fingers. Sally still bleating down phone but have gone deaf. Can only hear card: *Could I nip round one day and get your books signed for my nephew? Tom.* Followed by private phone number.

Most exquisite postcard ever, of course: Durer drawing of primroses. Heart throbs like billy-oh. Tell myself I am a matron and should cease this foolishness. Call Spouse, leave Sally, still talking, on hall table and smuggle my treasure into study. Read postcard forty-six times and seems more wonderful each time. Lift receiver and am poised to dial private number when Harriet runs in and says, 'Mummy! Come quick! It's boiling over!'

Down, wantons, down. Put tantalising young plumber's postcard in drawer and shut firmly. He wants to come round and get book autographed – at time convenient to me. Not first time I have received such a request from person of opposite sex. Nothing remarkable about it. Will probably slip my mind till end of next week. Got the whole thing in proportion, now. PMT to blame. Have often noticed how it puts the whore back into hormones.

Issue in new era of matronly responsibility by blowing dust off cookery book and making *Pollo Cacciatore*. Realise it is months since I made anything that aspired to a name. As usual bored by cookery book as no real characters in it – though intrigued by idea of Charlotte Russe. Better name for heroine than Charlotte Beaminster. Wonder if I shall ever manage to get to grips with gelatine before I die.

Spouse and children arrive, lured by scent of real food. 'Ugh not Italian muck!' shouts Henry. Spouse peers incredulously into casserole and asks what I am feeling guilty about.

Quickly confess that seed potatoes still unplanted. Spouse suggests soothingly that perhaps a local lad can be persuaded to do it. Do not wish to examine concept of local lad too closely as fear it may be unsettling. Suspect I may be succumbing to A.E. Housman syndrome: young male beauty Wrekin havoc with middle-aged literati.

Spouse offers weekend in London soon if we can get rid of the children somehow. Tortured by brief vision of young plumber dropping in whilst we are away. Banish vision and accept Spouse's offer gratefully, but fear it may not be enough to keep me on the path of matronly responsibility.

Announce establishment of compost heap and place bucket by sink for peelings, etc. Harriet asks why. Explain concept of Biodegradable, and tell her that we are all, too. Harriet bursts into tears, seizes my thigh and forbids me to biodegrade before bedtime. Alas – fear I have already broken down into fine tilth. Co-op carrier bags will inherit the earth.

Sit down to unusually good dinner. Halfway through *Pollo Cacciatore*, recall that I have not thought about young plumber for an hour and a half. Congratulate myself. Then lose appetite. Move bits of *Pollo Cacciatore* about on plate. Seems to be more now than when I started. Spouse notices and says if I don't want it he'll have it, and what's wrong with me anyway? Confess to feeling a little sick. Henry says, 'Are you going to actually be sick, Mummy? Great! Can we come and watch?'

Doorbell rings, at which cold nuclear fusion takes place in ribcage. Catapulted from chair by conviction it is Young Plumber. On way to front door notice hands look old. Dart into Futility Room where moisturiser, along with bird's nest and old cuckoo clock, repose in laundry basket. Squeeze tube. Enormous custard yellow dollop of moisturiser leaps into palm with disgusting noise. Enough to relieve dessicated elephant. Run to door wringing hands noisily.

Seize doornob, but slips through fingers. Cannot get purchase. Belatedly realise that key to human happiness is appropriate level of lubrication. Recall shrieking hinges, parties at which wine has run out, etc. Doorbell rings again, but doornob still elusive. Cry out, 'Just a minute – I'm having a bit of trouble with the door!' with what I hope is musical and lighthearted elan.

Wipe hands on skirt – a moment's desperation resulting in expenditure of £2.50 at dry cleaners – and have cornered doornob when phone rings. Call out 'You answer it!' hoping it will preoccupy Spouse whilst I have magic moment on doorstep with Young Plumber. Fling door open and bestow smile of radiant delight on Mrs Twill selling flags in aid of starving millions. Try to sustain expression of intense delight and hope it is not inappropriate.

Return forlornly to kitchen. Spouse is picking teeth and looking as if he expects a pudding. Offer choc ices, received by children with rapture and by Spouse with resignation. 'Oh, by the way,' says Spouse, 'that plumber Johnnie rang to ask if he'd left his spanner here. Doesn't know his arse from his elbow.'

Refrain from comment, but set myself simple task till bedtime: confine my thoughts to plumber's elbow.

Charlotte Beaminster walked into the plantation. Blindly, quiveringly, following her –
'Mummeeee! Can I have some crisps?'
'No! It's nearly lunchtime!'
Following her ... er ... no, wait, – the cruel thorns pierced her thin kid slippers but she was impelled towards –
'Snot fair! I hate you!' SLAM!
the leafy dell where she glimpsed Cherbagov's broad back. He was planting.

Oh hell! *Planting!* The seed potatoes! Burst from study like bat out of hell, seize spade and thrash nettles therewith. Then dig. Stung several times before conquering lazy urge to do without gardening gloves. Go to garage and find pile of gloves, originally pairs, but now promiscuously entangled in commune. Thrust fingers into one and encounter something tickly and alive. Scream and run away into house.

Encounter Spouse and Harriet looking bad-tempered and hungry. Have oft wished at such times they lived in a pit and I could throw them a bun or two at feeding time. Spouse enquires what I was thinking of for lunch. Diverted at idea I should think of lunch at all, and run upstairs to loo. Pursued by Harriet saying she wants a pee too she wants a pee first. Just manage to shut door in her face, at which she roars a threat to pee on carpet. Realise with sinking feeling that I have cystitis.

Another of Aphrodite's jokes. Repentance without pleasure. Have not had cystitis since honeymoon. Remember Siena – just. Harriet goes quiet on landing and I realise she is ransacking my handbag, which I know is full of toxic waste. Place head between knees and wish I was in the Campo, the Duomo ... indeed anywhere except 196 Cranford Gardens, Rusbridge.

Emerge and rescue bag from Harriet, or Harriet from bag. Brace myself, peer within and behold old matchbox containing two applecores (saved for compost heap); sheaf of evangelical literature I was too polite to refuse in the street, and increasingly dog-eared passport. All liberally scattered with aspirins as 'childproof' lid has evidently come off bottle.

Go downstairs and inform spouse I have cystitis and must go to the doctor. Spouse expects it's that bloody bidet. Seems to have taken a violent dislike to it. Even at this moment, manage – heroically – not to think about dashing young plumber.

'*What is this tree?*' *asked Charlotte, running her long white fingers down the rough bark.*

'*Pinus Sempervirens.*' *Cherbagov's deep, masterful tones vibrated in the tiny balls of Charlotte's Fabergé earrings, causing them to tinkle.*

'Lets grab some lunch at the pub, then,' says Spouse. Pluck

Henry from sofa where he is watching interminable video of cat and mouse decapitating, crucifying and flaying each other. America's idea of Fun for Kids.

At surgery, am unable to provide specimen so take bottle away to fill later. Go to pub and sit in draughty garden because of children. Leave Spouse to order from pretentious menu whilst I dash to loo with bottle. Whilst attempting to secure specimen, experience worst pang yet of penis envy. Also – blind hostility of fate – loo has run out of paper. Personally I would rather have *Papier pour le cu* than *Coq au Vin* any day, but not sure Spouse would agree. Slip bottle into handbag and return to find children devouring *Les Doigts de Poisson avec Haricots de Heinz*.

Toy listlessly with strange pie, into which many disagreeable vegetables and parts of dead body have been persuaded uneasily to co-exist. Wonder if I am really ill. Remember must drink large quantities. Wonder how much Perrier I could take before exploding. *Charlotte Beaminster felt Cherbagov's hot breath on her face* – sod off, Charlotte! You don't know you're born. Hatch devilish plot to give her cystitis in Chapter Sixteen.

Henry suddenly picks nose and eats it. *Morceaux de Nez*. Am in mid-tirade when Harriet upsets whole glass of orange juice over newly-ironed dress. Am just thinking *Nothing worse can happen* when, mopping up too enthusiastically, I knock half a pint of Perrier into my own lap.

Delve miserably into handbag for hankie, and am arrested by strangely softened and blurred appearance of passport. Realise with horror that specimen bottle has leaked all over it. Am begging Aphrodite to have mercy when who should walk into pub garden but dashing young plumber, accompanied by young girl of devastating beauty.

VYMURA: THE SHADE CARD POEM

♦

Liz Lochhead

Now artistic I aint, but I went to choose paint
'cos the state of the place made me sick.
I got a shade card, consumers-aid card, but it stayed hard to
  pick.
So I asked her advice as to what would look nice,
would blend in and not get on my wick.

She said 'our Vymura is super in Durer,
or see what you think of this new shade, Vlaminck.
But I see that you're choosy . . .
Picasso is newsy . . . that's greyish-greeny-bluesy . . .
Derain's all the rage . . .
that's hot-pink and Fauve-ish . . .
There's Monet . . . that's mauve-ish . . .
And Schwitters,
that's sort-of-a-*beige*.'

She said 'Fellow next door just sanded his floor
and rollered on Rouault and Rothko
His hall, och it's Pollock an' he
did his lounge in soft Hockney
with his cornice picked out in Kokoshka.'

'Now avoid the Van Gogh, you'll not get it off,
the Bonnard is bonny,
you'd be safe with matt Manet,
the Goya is *gorgeous*
or Chagall in eggshell,
but full-gloss Lautrec's sort of tacky.
So stick if you can to satin-finish Cezanne
or Constable ... that's kind of khaki.
Or the Gainsborough green ...
and I'd call it hooey to say Cimabue
would never tone in with Soutine.'

'If it looks a bit narrow when you splash on Pissarro
one-coat Magritte covers over.'
She said 'this Hitchens is a nice shade for kitchens
with some Ernst to connect 'em at other end of the spectrum,
Botticelli's lovely in the louvre.
She said 'If it was mine I'd do it Jim Dine ...
don't think me elitist or snobby ...
but Filipo Lippi'd
look awfy insipid,
especially in a large-ish lobby!'

Well, I did one wall Watteau, with the skirting Giotto,
and the door and the pelmet in Poussin.
The ceiling's de Kooning,
other walls all in Hals
and the whole place looks quite ... cavalier,
with the woodwork in Corot –
but I think tomorrow
I'll flat-white it back to Vermeer.

HEARTBURN

(AN EXTRACT)

———————— ♦ ————————

Nora Ephron

There were two reasons I didn't want to marry Mark. First of all, I didn't trust him. And second of all, I'd already been married. Mark had already been married, too, but that didn't really count; it certainly didn't count in the way it usually counts, which is that it makes you never want to get married again. Mark's first wife was named Kimberly. (As he always said, she was the first Jewish Kimberly.) Mark and Kimberly were married for less than a year, but he had enough material from her to last a lifetime. 'My wife, the first Jewish Kimberly,' Mark would begin, 'was so stingy that she made stew out of leftover pancakes.' Or: 'My wife, the first Jewish Kimberly, was so stingy she once tried to sell a used nylon stocking to a mugger.' In truth, the first Jewish Kimberly really was stingy, she recycled everything, and she once blew up their apartment and most of what was in it while making brandy out of old cherry pits.

My first husband was stingy, too, but that was the least of it. My first husband was so neurotic that every time he had an appointment, he erased the record of it from his datebook, so that at the end of the year his calendar was completely blank. My first husband was so neurotic he kept hamsters. They all had cute names, like Arnold and Shirley, and he was very attached to them and was always whipping up little salads for them with his Slice-o-Matic and buying them extremely small sweaters at a pet boutique in Rego Park. My first husband was so neurotic he would never eat fish because he'd once choked on a fishbone, and he would never eat onions because he claimed he was allergic to them, which he wasn't. I know, because I snuck them into everything. You can't really cook without onions. 'Is this an onion?' Charlie would say, his eyes narrowing as he held up a small, translucent object he had discovered floating in the sauce that covered his boneless dinner. 'No, it's a celery,' I would say. It didn't really fool him; at the end of every meal he would leave a neat little pile of small, translucent objects on his plate. God, was he neat. My first husband was so neat he put hospital corners on the newspaper he lined the hamster cage with.

The reason my marriage to Charlie broke up – although by now you're probably astonished that it lasted even a minute – was not because he slept with my oldest friend Brenda or even that he got crabs from her. It was because Arnold died. I felt really sad when Arnold died, because Charlie was devoted to Arnold and had invented a fairly elaborate personality for Arnold that Arnold did his best to live up to. Hamsters don't really do that much, but Charlie had built an entire character for Arnold and made up a lot of hamster jokes he claimed Arnold had come up with, mostly having to do with chopped lettuce. Also, and I'm sorry to tell you this, Charlie often talked in a high, squeaky voice that was meant to be Arnold's, and I'm even sorrier to tell you that I often replied in a high, squeaky voice that was meant to be Shirley's. You enter into a certain amount of madness when you marry a person with pets, but I didn't care. When Charlie and I were married, I was twenty-five years and eleven months old, and I was such a ninny that I thought: 'Thank God I'm getting married now, before I'm twenty-six and washed up.'

Anyway, when Arnold the hamster died, Charlie took him to one of those cryogenic places and had him frozen. It wasn't at all expensive, because the body was so small, on top of which there wasn't any additional charge for storage because

Charlie brought Arnold home in a nice Baggie with a rubber band around it and simply stuck him into the freezer. I could just see Cora Bigelow, the maid, taking Arnold out one Thursday thinking he was a newfangled freeze-dried potato treat in a boil bag; boy, would Charlie be in for a shock the next time he went to put an eensy-weensy bouquet of flowers next to Arnold's final resting place, directly to the right of the ice cube tray. I mean, what are you supposed to do with a first husband like that? I'll tell you what: divorce him. I'll tell you something else: when you divorce a first husband like that, you never look back. You never once think: 'God, I wish Charlie were here, he'd know how to handle this.' Charlie never handled anything if he could help it. He just made a note of it in his Mark Cross datebook and erased it when the problem had cleared up.

I left Charlie after six years, although at least two of those years were spent beating a dead horse. There have always been many things you can do short of actually ending a bad marriage – buying a house, having an affair and having a baby are the most common, I suppose – but in the early 1970s there were at least two more. You could go into consciousness raising and spend an evening a week talking over cheese to seven other women whose marriages were equally unhappy. And you could sit down with your husband and thrash everything out in a wildly irrelevant fashion by drawing up a list of household duties and dividing them up all over again. This happened in thousands of households, with identical results: thousands of husbands agreed to clear the table. They cleared the table. They cleared the table and then looked around as if they deserved a medal. They cleared the table and then hoped they would never again be asked to do another thing. They cleared the table and hoped the whole thing would go away. And it did. The women's movement went away, and so, in many cases, did their wives. Their wives went out into the world, free at last, single again, and discovered

BABY RULES

◆

Laurie Graham

Before we go any further – for those of you for whom it's not too late – are you quite sure you know what you're doing? Do you really want to have children? Or are you faking it? Might you not be happier with a timeshare apartment in the Algarve and a cupboard full of handmade shoes?

Let me tell you what's bothering me. There are lots of dumb reasons for having children. You might be thinking of it because your mother is sitting, moist-eyed, with idle knitting pins. You might be doing it out of providence, to fill the years ahead with purpose – acne and arguments and anorexia stored up in Kilner jars as insurance against lonely old age. Or dumbest of all, you might want to prove to the world that parenthood is as easy as falling off a log. Don't do it. Legions have gone before you, equipped with carrycots and optimism, prepared to show that a few kids needn't change anyone's lifestyle, and that one small baby need not deprive anyone of night life, good looks or an Ideal Home. They all finished up with Farex on their trousers.

Babies change everything. I don't care how smart you are. They are smarter. They are also relentless. An arrangement of mouth, bottom and terry towelling that runs away with the years and gives you nothing in return but indiscriminate, unconditional love. Are you still sure?

Then you must consider the details. Like how many, and

when. And who's going to look after them. Are you going to be contented with A Child or go for bust and have Children? If you decide that one is enough, you will have what is known in the business as An Only Child. And he has a folklore all of his own.

Did you know, for instance, that the Only Child is precocious, passive, introspective, selfish and socially inept? Haven't you heard that they grow into insufferable egotists and unaccountable odd-balls? Think back to your school days. Think of the ones who had calfskin attaché cases when everyone else had duffle bags, and the ones who weren't allowed to play in the street because they might have scuffed their shoes or got murdered. Weren't they all Only Children? *Not necessarily*.

As a mother of zillions I must speak up for the Only Child. I was one, am one myself. So are lots of my dearest friends, and a kinder, more lovable bunch a girl couldn't ask for. If their lack of brothers and sisters shows at all, it is in the importance they attach to relationships beyond their immediate family. They hardly ever wish things had been different. They've seen how shabbily brothers and sisters can treat one another.

Don't let anyone put you off having just one child. Provided he's not wrapped in mothballs, he's likely to grow into a perfectly decent sort, and when they've carted you and your photograph albums off to the Twilight Home, at least he won't refuse to come and visit you because he's not speaking to his sister and his brother's wife isn't speaking to anyone.

He'll be cheaper, quieter and faster to mature. He'll become accustomed at an early age to adult conversation and solitude and, if you are the sort of people who won't be able to resist pandering to his every whim, it will be very much easier to do it for one than it will to do it for lots.

Of course, the best laid plans can go wrong. You may intend to have one and end up with more.

Two at a time is called twins, more than two is called a

nightmare. If anything like this happens to you you're not going to find a lot of time for reading, so I'll keep this short and to the point.

When it first happens people will be jolly nice about it. They'll rush around borrowing extra high chairs from nodding acquaintances and keep telling you to go and put your feet up for an hour. For about six weeks you will nearly drown in the milk of human kindness, and then suddenly everyone will disappear. The novelty of your conveyor belt existence will have worn off, and you will be left alone with the massed voices of hunger, grizzle and shitty despair.

No one will care that you haven't been able to get out of your housecoat all week. Your house will be littered with mugs of cold coffee and lists of things you're going to do some day; and from time to time a grey, unshaven wreck will shuffle by, to knock over one of those cold coffees and demand that most basic of conjugal privileges, a blazing row.

When you eventually find the time to zip up your slacks and hit the road, total strangers will stop you everywhere you go to tell you what a perfect picture your little family makes, and how they would have loved to have had triplets themselves. Here is what you should do. Put the three-seater buggy firmly in their hands, and offer to send the rest of the luggage on later. They will then laugh nervously, and tell you you can't mean it. Don't be put off by this fickle change of tune. Give them your address and tell them you have sixty little nails to trim on bath night and are not too proud to accept the help of someone who always wanted triplets.

If you've got more than three, people will talk not so much *to* you as *about* you. They'll go into huddles in Boots to give each other the lowdown on how much *Woman's Own* paid for your story, and how many cartons of babycare freebies you've got stashed in your garage. 'Of course,' they'll say tartly, 'they've made an absolute mint out of those quads.'

On the positive side of multiple parenthood, you will have the bonus of instant family chumminess. And later you will find that you have new strengths that come of surviving Trial by Ordeal. And, if ever you feel inclined to look for paid work, you'll find the world is crying out for man-managers of your calibre. You'll be pretty hot at juggling as well.

I'll leave it there. In the two minutes it's taken you to read that, at least one of your babies must be halfway up the stairs with her brother in her mouth and you'll need to be getting on. Just remember that there are lots of us out here willing you to survive. We'll see you in about five years' time.

We boring types who pod out one at a time have to decide for ourselves the size of our folly. You may be adding a thing or two, a wing or two. It comes down to this. How tired and poor are you prepared to be, and for how long? If you have your children close together, the exhaustion will be extreme but it will be over faster, leaving you a clear run of about twenty years for wild parties, adult movies and still being awake for *News at Ten*, before they start lumbering you with the grandchildren and it starts all over again. If you space them wider, your body will have time to recover from each assault, and then, just as it's nodded off into normality you'll spring it the ugly surprise of another stint on the night shift. It depends which you're better at, sprints or hurdles.

Three years is a favourite gap. I shall never understand why. A three-year-old is a loathsome thing. Ideally it should be put in a deep freeze until it is of school age. If you introduce it to a new brother or sister, it will aspire at once to new heights of loathsomeness. It will help you by talcum powdering the whole house. It will demand breast milk with menaces and, when you offer it your spare breast, it will run away and play its xylophone all afternoon. And it will completely forget that it ever knew what a potty was for.

Younger than three they are too ga-ga to notice that you've slipped another one in. Later on they may ask but you can just say, 'Abigail? She's your sister. She's been here for years.'

From about five onwards children can be very nice about newcomers. They show genuine affection and pride where the baby is concerned, are nearly always willing to humour anyone who is hot and bored with being six months old, and they can be very helpful about fetching and carrying for you.

Girls are especially good at this age. With boys it comes later. If you're planning on having a teenager and a baby in the same family, let the teenager be a boy. Teenage boys are gentle, solicitous and generally wonderful about pregnancy and babies. Don't be surprised if your house is suddenly full of lurking lads with lovely bodies and horrible complexions. These are your son's friends and they are willing to help. Let them. They can make you a cup of tea, or allow your golden retriever to take them for a walk, and you can reward them with the Dial-a-Pizza of their choice.

If your teenager is a girl it will be a very different story. She'll start complaining as soon as she knows you're pregnant, and she won't let up. About how she can never hold her head up again because it's so gross, so embarrassing. She'll be worried about the baby waking her because she'll be at an age when she really needs her sleep, what with CSEs and having to stay up till all hours piercing each other's ears and pitying people who are over twenty. And you needn't think she's stopping in to babysit for you, because she's not. She has become a hunter of men. Well, not strictly men. Rather, a slightly sweatier, more knowing version of the ones who like holding babies and chatting to lactating old ladies. Like all predators, she doesn't have a lot of time for hanging around. A snatched three hours in the bathroom, re-applying the Pan-Stik and she'll need to be back out there on Mean Street, sniffing for trouser and taking no prisoners.

Probably the best thing is not to tell her at all. She won't notice the pregnancy because she thinks you're obscenely fat anyway. If she notices anything after the birth, just tell her it's something you've borrowed for a few days. No need to burden her with the details. By the time you get to the word 'borrowed', she will have switched on her Walkman.

As for numbers, the more you have, the higher your running costs, but not proportionately so. Things get handed on and made over, and, somehow, the bigger the family, the more cheerful everyone is about being scruffy. And the more of you there are to huddle together on a bleak winter's night, the less you'll spend on coal. There's no escaping the fact that eight people eat more than four people, but they do not necessarily eat twice as much, and there is a lot less waste.

The advantages of the larger family is that it is far less labour-intensive. Parents of one or two children always seem to work a lot harder to achieve the same results. They have no sooner settled themselves with the *News of the World* and a Duncan's Walnut Whip than there is a child standing before them with Snakes and Ladders and a look of wistful loneliness. Where there are two children and two parents there is an unspoken assumption that you will pair off, either in the modern fashion with the sexes crossed, or in traditional style, with the women icing biscuits and the men grouting tiles.

In a large family you get a much better mix. There's always someone around to play Ludo or have a quarrel with you, and everyone can have a turn at being a good sport, or an unapproachable grouch.

Nowadays four is considered a large family, but three is not. More than four is reckoned to be a symptom of Catholicism, insanity, or an ancient and aristocratic pedigree. Unlike the newly rich, who settle for two children and a well-maintained suntan, old money likes to have lots of children. That way they get plenty of wear and tear out of everything they buy, they have a better chance of keeping warm when the wind whistles through the east wing, and they are never short of good homes for all those silver spoons and ugly sideboards they are honoured to own.

You may have some limited control over how many children and their age differences, but you are stuck with who they are and what they think of one another. There is likely to be one relationship that grates. You can't do anything about it except hope for improvement or emigration when they get to adulthood. Some brothers and sisters will never like one another. But, in general, the question of who hates whom will go in phases.

Nine-year-old boys for instance, are not very highly rated by thirteen-year-old girls. But when that thirteen-year-old was nine and her brother was five, there's every chance that they were the best of friends. The scene shifts endlessly, so no problem need be with you for long. Just remember that the more biddable the girl when she is young, the louder the hysterics when she grows up; that cockiness in the pre-pubescent boy gives way eventually to introspection and stubble on the chin; and that in each generation, every family worth its salt throws up one misanthropic crab. The fact that yours has freckles and a ponytail does not mean that the rest of the world is wrong and she is right.

Some children get out of bed the wrong side the very first day, and that's the way they stay. If by a cruel trick of genetics you find yourself with more than one of these characters in your family, you should insist that they bunk down in the same room, and get yourself the best earplugs money can buy.

When you've got them, who is going to look after them? Will one of you stay home, for a year or two, or ten? Or will you pay someone a lot of money to bring them up for you? And, if you're united in the view that one of you should stick around for the formative years, who is it going to be?

Whichever of you it is, you're not going to be doing it for ever. If you're a man you probably already have a very clear idea of how long you're going to do it for and what you're going to do afterwards. If you're a woman your plans are likely to be much more vague. Get the youngest one settled in school and then see about doing something? Something different as like as not because you never felt really *galvanised* by food technology, and you'd actually quite like to study Arabic. Some day.

There are things you should know about Life After Small Children. The first is this. If there's even the remotest chance that you'll want to take a break and then go back to the work you did before, *keep your hand in*. Do a bit of part time, put yourself about, and copy the boys, by hanging on to every slightly useful contact you ever make. If you don't, round about your thirty-second birthday you will start to become invisible, and by thirty-five there will be less left of you than there was of the Cheshire Cat. I don't care how marvellous everyone said you were in 1979.

Of course you might not want to go back. You might want a complete change. To retrain. Or set up your own business. The second thing you should know is this: *beware of pretending*. Just as reading articles in *Good Housekeeping* on quick, delicious meals for working mothers is not the same as being a working mother and coming home to a tin of cornflour and a bag of frozen peas, so having a go at a few pressed flower pictures is not the same as opening your own craft shop.

After years of wiping a nose as you scramble the eggs as you answer the telephone and say no to the Avon lady through the window, it is difficult to settle to sustained concentration on one thing. And that's what you will have to do if you're going to study or create or innovate. You will have to become selfish, demanding, and at times, completely unavailable. And that's not very nice, is it?

If you are going to be the one who goes out every morning and comes home most evenings, in the eyes of your children you will be a magical figure. They'll look forward to the sound of your key in the door and they'll hug you a lot. A lot more than if you'd been there all afternoon making gingerbread men or upstairs, with your oil paints and a heavy cupboard against your door, shouting 'I'm not here!'

If you do something interesting, like working in a toy shop, or cutting the hair of someone whose brother used to live next door to Ian Rush, your children will also be very proud and approving. If you're a working father this may give you no more passing pleasure. But, if you are a working mother, such approval will mean a lot to you. Your children may give it gladly, but the rest of the world will not. School will be politely chilly about it, Granny will be pained to hear that the children's coughs never seem to get any better, and Society will be prepared to blame you for everything, from Junk Food to the Militant Tendency.

The other thing that happens to you when you have children is that you are bound to have more to do with other people's children. A lot of it will be unavoidable. At first there will be the children your family and close friends have produced. Later the circle will widen. There will be neighbours' children, school friends and eventually your own grandchildren. Please remember you are not obliged to like any of them.

If you have no children yourself, other people's babies are not very interesting. If you're busy revising for your Bar finals, or establishing goodwill and a paying clientele for your mobile chiropody service, the number of teeth your nephew can boast will not be as riveting as your sister may suggest it should be.

But, if you have a young family yourself, you'll really be into teeth. And stretch marks. And wipeable surfaces. It can be very cosy, a lot of you with youngsters of about the same age. So much will not need to be explained. The little dollops of used kitchen paper behind the settee. Not being able to use the front door because the pram is in the way. And the way you keep falling asleep in the middle of a sentence.

There will be so much to talk about. Natural childbirth can last a whole dinner party. The man you would have sworn was smarter than Jeffrey Archer will talk foetal monitoring all the way through to the crème brulée with the man everyone said was funnier than Miles Kington. At times like these it's good to be among friends.

It changes the day one of the juniors takes his first step. The minute he's on the move you will start to discover what a menace children can be, especially when they belong to people you always thought were your friends.

There are two common mistakes. One is to think that because you like the parents you will also like the child. The other is to suppose that you can all carry on the way you used to. Grown-ups together, laughing, arguing, drinking each other's undrinkable wine and hardly being interrupted at all by the chaps in the terry snuggle suits. No one wants to have to stop halfway through every sentence to say, 'Take that out of your mouth, Tobias.' No one wants to leave their chilli to go cold while they step outside to make Prudence see reason.

The sad truth is that small, mobile children and the normal social life of a friendly adult are incompatible. You ask old friends round for a game of Mah Jong and a Peking Garden dinner for six, and what happens? They bring Jake with them. He pulls all the books off your shelves and they are so busy telling you about their Bargain Break Weekend in Amsterdam that they don't even notice. They bring along a jaunty collapsible cot, and he refuses to collapse in it. A stripy leg keeps appearing over the side, and he will still be up at midnight, dribbling all over the prawn crackers. Before the sun rises, you will hate him. You have known his parents for years. You would have staked your life on their knowing how to handle Jake. And now here he is, swinging from your Swiss cheese plant and calling you Nunkie.

What do you do? Put up with it in the name of friendship and then swear a lot after they've gone home? Rip them out of your address book? Or take them to one side and tell them, 'Tim, Patsie, we go back a long way so we know you'll thank us for telling you that Becky is not welcome to sit on her potty during our poker games. We'll call you again when she's left home.'

Brave words! Are you really up to that sort of performance? I'm not. I love my friends and I want to keep them.

As their children get older and your children get older, the friendship will be put well and truly to the test. One of theirs will fight with one of yours and you will be asked to act as referee. Each will say the other started it, cross their hearts and hope to die, and you'll end up blaming your own kid for everything that's gone wrong that day, from the breakdown in East–West relations to the fact that the fire has gone out. After your friends have gone, you can apologise until you're blue in the face, but your child will have learned something he will never forget. That visiting children get away with daylight robbery. And that blood is not necessarily thicker than water.

Your children will get to know which visitors to dread. I think it helps to be honest. Tell them you know what they go through. A word or two about stiff upper lips. It won't hurt them. Wherever they go in life there's going to be someone waiting to jump on their train set.

Friendship is one thing. Neighbourliness is quite another. If your neighbours have children of an age with your own, you will find that their relationship with one another will be one of extremes. They will either live in each other's houses, swapping their most prized possessions, dressing identically and begging not to be parted even for eight hours of essential sleep; or it will be all-out war: verbal abuse, party invitations rescinded, and footballs not thrown back over the garden fence. Talking of fences, I recommend nothing less than six feet. All the way round.

If war is declared, you'll find girls are worse than boys. Boys have a quick wrestle in the gutter, the winner goes home to crow, the loser goes home for Elastoplast and they're back out there on their pogo sticks by next morning, the very best of friends. Girls go on for weeks. Writing notes. Lobbying for useful support. And watching carefully for that special moment when they know they can negotiate from a position of advantage. It beats me why more of them don't go into politics when they grow up.

As parents, what you are not supposed to do is get involved. This is a modern, middle-class convention. In olden times women were for ever out on their doorsteps exchanging compliments. It was a cheap and wholesome form of entertainment. If you thought your neighbour's child was a venomous, scabby-kneed doughball, you could say so, loud enough for it to be generally broadcast, and not be the least surprised to hear that your own pet lamb was a raggy-arsed thief who probably took after his father if only anyone knew who his father was. Now we are supposed to be above that sort of degrading behaviour. It is considered more fitting to plump the cushions and say pleasantly, 'I expect you'll be friends again soon.' But mark my words. No good ever came out of such repression. Small wonder there's so much psoriasis on these new estates.

Your neighbours may not be your friends. Why should they be? Just because your houses are stuck together is no reason for there to be a deep and meaningful relationship between you. Where I grew up it was absolutely understood that no one had a kind word to say for anyone. If you broke your leg, they fetched your shopping in for you, and if you died, they collected for a wreath, but that was as far as it went. And if there was trouble between children, there was a great putting on of coats over pinnies, and hammering on doors with offers of bodily violence from one absent husband to another.

Other people's children *can* be fascinating. They can make you realise things about your own children, like how nice they are. They can jolt you into asking yourself questions, such as 'Am I turning my children into social pariahs by allowing them to use the word *bum*?' and 'Does my lavatory cleaner *really* get right up under the rim?' Other people's children can give you titillating glimpses of what goes on behind closed doors. Some children look at you in such startled terror when you ask them if they'd like an egg sandwich that you realise no adult has ever spoken to them politely before. Some just run up and down stairs and bang doors a lot, without even seeming to notice you. These are the ones with timid, low-profile parents whose hearing is not what it used to be.

Some will eat nothing but chips. Some have never seen fresh fruit. And some will arrive with their carpet slippers, their own towel and a disposable medicated cover to put over your lavatory seat.

One or two will arrive uninvited. This happens a lot when your child first starts school. He turns up with total strangers who tell you they are allergic to cheap beefburgers. Or three weeks before his birthday you hear that he has personally invited all forty of his classmates to his party. You then have the thankless job of dealing out invitations to the favoured few and dealing with anxious enquiries from the reserve list and their mothers.

The ones you do invite will give you the largest dose of other people's children you are ever likely to have to swallow. Most of them will be there because your child went to their party, duty coming before pleasure even for the very young. One or two will be there because of bribery, string-pulling and spontaneous goodwill. The best ones of all are the accomplished party-goers. They know how to ask for the toilet. They are not shy of any strange adults you may have hanging around, like aunts with teeth that click or grandads that do the twist. And, when it's time to go home, they know exactly which coat is theirs, and how to line up for a balloon on a string and to say Thankyouforhavingme.

I've met about a dozen children like this in years of looking, and thousands of the other sort.

Like I said, get a six-foot fence.

COLD COMFORT FARM

(AN EXTRACT)

◆

Stella Gibbons

Adam had finished slicing turnips and had gone out into the yard, where a thorn-tree grew, and returned with a long thorn-spiked twig torn from its branches. Flora watched him with interest while he turned the cold water on to the crusted plates, and began picking at the incrustations of porridge with his twig.

She bore it as long as she could, for she could hardly believe her own eyes, and then she said: 'What on earth are you doing?'

'Cletterin' the dishes, Robert Poste's child.'

'But surely you could do it much more easily with a little mop? A nice little mop with a handle? Cousin Judith ought to get you one. Why don't you ask her? It would get the dishes cleaner, and it would be so much quicker, too.'

'I don't want a liddle mop wi' a handle. I've used a thorn twig these fifty years and more, and what was good enough then is good enough now. And I don't want to cletter the dishes more quickly, neither. It passes the time away, and takes me thoughts off my liddle wild bird.'

'But,' suggested the cunning Flora, remembering the conversation which had roused her that morning at dawn, 'if you had a little mop and could wash the dishes more quickly, you could have more time in the cowshed with the dumb beasts.'

Adam stopped his work. This had evidently struck home.

He nodded once or twice, without turning round, as though he were pondering it; and Flora hastily followed up her advantage.

'Anyway, I shall buy one for you when I go into Beershorn to-morrow.'

... Flora was quite enjoying herself. She was mixed up in a good many plots. Only a person with a candid mind, who is usually bored by intrigues, can appreciate the full fun of an intrigue when they begin to manage one for the first time. If there are several intrigues and there is a certain danger of their getting mixed up and spoiling each other, the enjoyment is even keener.

Of course, some of the plots were going better than others. Her plot to make Adam use a little mop to clean the dishes with, instead of a thorn twig, had gone sour on her.

One day, when Adam came into the kitchen just after breakfast, Flora had said to him: 'Oh, Adam, here's your little mop. I got it in Howling this afternoon. Look, isn't it a nice little one? You try it and see.'

For a second she had thought he would dash it from her hand, but gradually, as he stared at the little mop, his expression of fury changed to one more difficult to read.

It was, indeed, rather a nice little mop. It had a plain handle of white wood with a little waist right at the tip, so that it could be more comfortably held in the hand. Its head was of soft white threads, each fibre being distinct and comely instead of being matted together in an unsightly lump like the heads of most little mops. Most taking of all, it had a loop of fine red string, with which to hang it up, knotted round its little waist.

Adam cautiously put out his finger and poked at it. ''Tes mine?'

'Aye – I mean, yes, it's yours. Your very own. Do take it.'

He took it between his finger and thumb and stood gazing

at it. His eyes had filmed over like sightless Atlantic pools before the flurry of the storm breath. His gnarled fingers folded round the handle.

'Aye ... 'tes mine,' he muttered. 'Nor house nor kine, and yes 'tes mine ... My little mop!'

He undid the thorn twig which fastened the bosom of his shirt and thrust the mop within. But then he withdrew it again, and replaced the thorn. 'My little mop!' He stood staring at it in a dream.

'Yes. It's to cletter the dishes with,' said Flora, firmly, suddenly foreseeing a new danger on the horizon.

'Nay ... nay,' protested Adam. ''Tes too pretty to cletter those great old dishes wi'. I mun do that with the thorn twigs; they'll serve. I'll keep my liddle mop in the shed, along wi' our Pointless and our Feckless.'

'They might eat it,' suggested Flora.

'Aye, aye, so they might, Robert Poste's child. Ah, well, I mun hang it up by its liddle red string above the dishwashin' bowl. Niver put my liddle pretty in that gurt old greasy washin'-up water. Aye, 'tes prettier nor apple-blooth, my liddle mop.'

And shuffling across the kitchen, he hung it carefully on the wall above the sink, and stood for some time admiring it. Flora was justifiably irritated, and went crossly out for a walk.

BEHAVING BADLY

♦

*Out of two evils I always choose the one I've never
tried before.*
Mae West

There is no point in growing old unless you can be a witch.
Germaine Greer

*The man who is a bigot
is the worst thing God has got,
except his match, his woman,
who really is Ms. Bigot.*
Maya Angelou

RE-ENTER MARGOT ASQUITH

Dorothy Parker

◆

October 22, 1927

'Daddy, what's an optimist?' said Pat to Mike while they were walking down the street together one day.

'One who thought that Margot Asquith* wasn't going to write any more,' replied the absent-minded professor, as he wound up the cat and put the clock out.

That gifted entertainer, the Countess of Oxford and Asquith, author of *The Autobiography of Margot Asquith* (four volumes, neatly boxed, suitable for throwing purposes), reverts to tripe in a new book deftly entitled *Lay Sermons*. It is a little dandy if I have ever seen one, and I certainly have.

I think it must be pleasanter to be Margot Asquith than to be any other living human being; and this is no matter of snap judgment on my part, for I have given long and envious thought to the desirability of being Charles A. Levine.† But the lady seems to have even more self-assurance than has the argumentative birdman. Her perfect confidence in herself is a thing to which monuments should be erected; hers is a poise that ought to be on display in the British Museum. The affair

* *Margot (Tennant) Asquith* (1864–1945), wife of the British Prime Minister of 1908–1916, was known as a wit in London literary and social circles.
† *Charles A. Levine* made headlines in 1927 by following a few days after Lindbergh in a nonstop transatlantic flight, with Clarence D. Chamberlain, which overshot Berlin.

between Margot Asquith and Margot Asquith will live as one of the prettiest love stories in all literature.

In this book of essays, which has all the depth and glitter of a worn dime, the Countess walks right up to such subjects as Health, Human Nature, Fame, Character, Marriage, Politics, and Opportunities. A rather large order, you might say, but it leaves the lady with unturned hair. Successively, she knocks down and drags out each topic. And there is something vastly stirring in the way in which, no matter where she takes off from, she brings the discourse back to Margot Asquith. Such singleness of purpose is met but infrequently.

When she does get around to less personal matters, it turns out that her conclusions are soothingly far from startling. A compilation of her sentiments, suitably engraved upon a nice, big calendar, would make an ideal Christmas gift for your pastor, your dentist, or Junior's music teacher. Here, for instance, are a few ingots lifted from her golden treasury: 'The artistic temperament has been known to land people in every kind of dilemma.' ... 'Pleasure will always make a stronger appeal than Wisdom.' ... 'It is only the fine natures that profit by Experience.' ... 'It is better to be a pioneer than a passenger, and best of all to try and create.' ... 'It is not only what you See but what you Feel that kindles appreciation and gives life to Beauty.' ... 'Quite apart from the question of sex, some of the greatest rascals have been loved.' ... 'I think it is a duty women owe not only to themselves, but to everyone else, to dress well.'

The Thames, I hear, remains as damp as ever in the face of these observations.

Through the pages of *Lay Sermons* walk the great. I don't say that Margot Asquith actually permits us to rub elbows with them ourselves, but she willingly shows us her own elbow, which has been, so to say, honed on the mighty. 'I remember President Wilson saying to me'; 'John Addington Symonds once said to me'; 'The Master of Balliol told me' – thus does she introduce her anecdotes. And you know those

anecdotes that begin that way; me, I find them more effi-
cacious than sheep-counting, rain on a tin roof, or alanol
tablets. Just begin a story with such a phrase as 'I remember
Disraeli – poor old Dizzy! – once saying to me, in answer to
my poke in the eye,' and you will find me and Morpheus off
in a corner, necking.

Margot Asquith's is, I am sure, a naive and an annoying
(those two adjectives must ever be synonyms to me) and an
unimportant book, yet somehow, grudge it though I do,
there is a disarming quality to it and to its author. (There I go,
getting tender about things, again; it's no wonder men forget
me.) Perhaps it is because the lady's cocksureness implies a
certain sort of desperate gallantry; perhaps it is because there
is a little – oh, entirely unconscious, please, Your Grace –
wistfulness in the recurrent references to the dear dead days
of 'The Souls,' in the tales of the hunting-field when the high
gentry were wont to exclaim, 'You ride with such audacity,
Miss Tennant!' I suppose that wistfulness is a fighting word
to the countess, but there it stands. She is, from her book, no
master mind, God wot; but she is, also from her book, a game
woman, gamer, I think, than she knows. I always have to cry a
little bit about courage.

However (and how good it feels to get back to the nice,
firm ground again), *Lay Sermons* is a naive and an annoying
and an unimportant book. The author says, 'I am not sure
that my ultimate choice for the name of this modest work is
altogether happy.' Happier I think it would have been if,
instead of the word 'Sermons,' she had selected the word
'Off.'

HELEN LEDERER

♦

Helen Lederer

It's great to be here. It really is very, very funny. It's a real privilege, actually, to be asked to come and perform free – especially so. Thanks. Lovely. In fact, I think I'm the only one. The rest are being paid, so I feel great. Thank you very much for making me feel so special.

Anyway, I haven't actually been very well recently, in case any of you were worried. I thought you might be. I thought I had ME, you know, the yuppie flu, so I went to the doctor, and I said, 'I think I've got yuppie flu,' you see.

So he said, 'How much do you earn?' So I told him and he said, 'Yes, you're just run down.'

I wasn't going to be fobbed off. I asked for some tests, but, being the NHS, they couldn't offer me an immediate appointment date, obviously, so what he offered to do was place my notes in a time capsule and conceal them under the surgery floorboards, which I thought was quite encouraging.

Anyway, well, I know what I've got, actually. I've got hormonal imbalance. It's quite a neat label. It's not a problem if you've got hormonal imbalance: it just means that you don't lay eggs, well, not to EC standards anyway, in case anyone wondered. People might need to know that. I don't know. It's peculiar to me, possibly. So what they do, you see, to address it, is they have to give you more hormones. I don't know where they get them from. I don't like to pry, actually.

They said it was from some laboratory in Switzerland. I think it was more like some sheep's bottom in the Lake District. That's what it smelt like.

The thing is, I know what the problem is. The real problem is I've just had a fling. I know, I was shocked. You see, what happened was the phone went in the house, and I answered it because I wasn't doing anything else, obviously, and the voice said, 'Hello! How would you like to come for a dirty week-end in Paris?' And then there was silence and the voice said, 'I'm sorry. Have I shocked you?'

And I said, 'God, no. I was just packing.'

It was great. It was really romantic. When I say romantic, actually, I found it quite difficult to get aroused, really I did, because some things are just passion killers. I mean, a man naked except for a pair of socks is completely repellent to me, and then it's worse when they take them off because then you get that elastic pattern round the ankles, quite ugly. No, it cuts both ways. I remember he commented on the size of my Caesarian scar, and then I had to say, 'No, it isn't one. It's just that this slip's too tight.' But he was a very considerate lover, to be fair. He insisted on lying on the damp patch afterwards. He was a real Sir Walter Raleigh.

Anyway, so I got back from Paris and I thought to myself, am I actually in a long-term relationship? You know, I was panicking, and I thought, I am. So I immediately got my Filofax and set aside six months for the inevitable post-break-up grief, December through till June, because you can get some away-breaks in June which I thought I might be needing. No, but I mean there were problems. He was obsessed with my age. He was always asking me how old I was, and in the end I told him, 'OK. I'm thirty ... something, thirty-something.' You know, like the soap opera. I haven't actually seen the soap opera, but I have seen the Gold Blend coffee ad, which I think is quite a good role model to use. Anyway he was obsessed, and when you're thirty-plus, you're just too old for balloons, aren't you? Well, unless they come in packets of three, I always say – bit of a joke there.

It was a very, very mature relationship. We insisted on giving each other lots of space. In fact, we might have over-done it. I phoned him up the other day, and I said, 'What have you been doing since our last date?'

And he said, 'Well, got married, had a couple of kids, you know.' But I'm comfortable with that because ... I *am*. Why shouldn't he have other female friends? I know I do.

HOT BREATH

(AN EXTRACT)

◆

Sarah Harrison

During dinner I had the sensation of things getting out of hand. For a start, I was tight. When nervous I drank fast, and the effects were delayed and catastrophic. Mike and Linda had been oiled to begin with and were now so well lubricated they were like a couple of cakes of soap – you couldn't grab hold of them. Crazily they slithered and swooped from one anecdote to the next, spilling salt, sending slivers of tomato and Spanish onion cascading to the ground to be sniffed and rejected by Fluffy, helping themselves to wine and periodically over-filling glasses and shouting 'whoops'. Their mood was infectious. The tenor of the party became one of febrile hilarity. Bernice's judo jacket sagged invitingly. Constantine's expression became a lot less polite. I caught Bernice's eye and treated her cleavage to a withering look. Obligingly she tweaked it, and it parted again.

During the syllabub the phone rang and I answered it.

'Is Dr Ghikas there?' asked a female voice, elderly and genteel.

'Yes, he is. Who is that?'

The voice frosted over. 'I was given this number by the surgery.'

'Just hang on – ' I put my hand over the mouthpiece. 'Constantine, it's for you.'

'Thank you – sorry about this.'

'Take it in the bedroom if you want to, top of the stairs and facing.'

I waited until I heard him lift the receiver, then put mine down and went back to the table.

'Poor bugger,' said Mike. 'Who'd be a doctor, eh?'

'I would,' said Bernice. 'You never see a doctor on a bike.'

'Oh yes, but *darling*,' protested Mike, 'what a life. Ghastly surgeries full of snotty kids and haemorrhoids and thread worm – '

'That's the nurse,' I corrected him. 'The nurse does thread worm.'

'Glad you told me that!' said Mike and we all laughed merrily.

'But fancy being on call at the weekend like this,' said Linda, in her best seriously-though tone. 'Like running a shop.'

We pondered this simile, and then Bernice said: 'He's gorgeous, though.'

'Oh *yes*,' agreed Linda. 'Tasty, tasty!'

'Don't be ridiculous,' I blustered, in the overemphatic way of the woman with the bad conscience.

'Never you mind, girl,' said Mike, putting his arm round me. 'Your secret is safe with us. A little field work, eh? A little research? And why the hell not!'

Constantine came back into the room and sat down in his place.

'That was quick!' observed Linda. 'Not terminal then?'

'No. She quite often rings me up.'

'Ah, hypochondriac is it . . . ?' asked Mike with the air of one versed in medical lore.

'No,' said Constantine, 'just elderly and on her own.'

This cast something of a blight. But Mike Channing on the outside of three g. and t.s and a bottle of Beaujolais would have been proof against an arctic blizzard.

'There was a young lady of Parva,' he declaimed, 'who had

an affair with her farver. She said, "Callow youth is so rough and uncouth, but Farver in Parva is suaver!"'

We all laughed immoderately, especially Mike, who had tears coursing down his cheeks. Constantine laughed in a slightly stupefied way as if he couldn't believe his eyes and ears. He had long since started covering his wine glass with his hand to preclude topping-up and I did hope the rest of us didn't seem too disgusting.

'How about a game?' asked Mike. 'Would anyone like to play a game?'

'God, Mike, really ... !' said Linda, 'I'm sure they don't.'

'I do!' said Bernice predictably.

'Good idea,' agreed Constantine, more surprisingly.

Mike looked at me. 'Harriet?'

I was overcome with a mild sense of hysteria. 'Sure, sure, why not ... ?'

'Attagirl!'

While I put on the kettle for coffee Mike herded his little flock back into the sitting room and began outlining the game.

As I stood there gazing into space and wondering where it would all lead, the back door opened and Damon came in.

'Perfect timing!' I cried. 'We've just finished and you can make the coffee. Four large spoonfuls in this jug, and don't forget to bring a strainer, out of this drawer.'

'Oh yeah. Right. Will do.' He removed his jacket and hung it on the back of one of the chairs. In my well-refreshed state I felt almost maternal towards him but when I smiled – benignly, as I thought – he shied away as though Count Dracula had treated him to a leer dripping with gore.

'Where are your kids?' he asked, as if to remind me of my respectable matronly status.

'Out,' I explained. 'Thank you, Damon, this really is a great help.'

''Sorlright, I got nothing on,' was his reply.

Back in the sitting room, a short reprise from Mike gave me

to understand that the game involved a man carrying a woman from point A to point B with various prescribed parts of her body touching the ground at all times.

'But who's the arbiter?' asked Bernice. 'I mean who says which parts?'

'We all write down different parts on bits of paper and put them in a hat or a bin or something, and someone makes a selection before each go,' said Mike. 'It's easy-peasy.'

'What's the object of the exercise?' asked Constantine, the last rational voice on earth.

'Just to do it!' replied Linda. 'Because It's There.'

'Well, not quite, darling,' said Mike. 'It will be over a set course and against the clock.'

'I see,' said Constantine.

'Right-ho then!' cried Bernice. 'What are we waiting for? Give me a pencil and paper, someone.'

I fetched both from the study and we all scribbled busily. Linda touched Constantine on the arm. 'Be careful, won't you, doctor,' she said. 'I don't want to end the evening with a prolapse.'

'Heaven forfend,' he murmured, deep in thought.

When we'd finished writing Bernice screwed up the bits of paper and put them in a vase, while Mike rummaged through George's tapes and put on Francis Albert.

'Songs for Swinging Naughty Bits,' he announced.

'There's a fly in this ointment,' observed Bernice. 'We're not an even number.'

'I could take two,' offered Constantine gamely, holding his glass of Perrier like a badge of office.

At this moment Damon came in with the coffee tray. Bernice rose from her chair with the suggestion of a lurch, and more than a suggestion of the swinging naughty bits to which Mike had but lately referred.

'Put the tray down, Damon,' she ordered. 'You *shall* go to the ball.' It was evidence of how drunk I was that beyond a slight peck of mild surprise I accepted this solution with equanamity.

'Could you lift me, Damon?' asked Bernice reflectively, looking him up and down. He was by three or four inches and twenty pounds the smallest person in the room, and not in rude health.

He eyed her back. 'Doubt it. I could try.'

Bernice waved a dismissive, imperious hand. 'For fuck's sake,' she said, 'it's 1984. I'll carry *him*.'

'Sure, fine, right, okay,' said Mike, impatient with the delay. 'Now who's going first?'

'You're the expert, you go first,' I said. 'You and Linda.'

'May I know where I am to be carried?' asked Linda.

'I hereby declare this fireplace point A and the front door point B,' said Mike. 'Any queries?'

'That's hellishly difficult,' complained Linda, taking off her shoes. 'We're all going to get wedged in this doorway.'

'That, petal, is where the skill comes in. The course is there and back, against the clock. Okey-dokey, allons-y!' He thrust his hand into the vase and brought it out clutching a bit of paper.

'It says here, left elbow.' He held the paper up for the rest of us to see. Then he scrutinised his wife, like a removal man assessing an awkward piece of furniture – a harp, a grand piano, a large and elaborate desk – and finally rushed her, in one movement turning her upside down with her head on the sofa, and wrapping her ankles round his neck. This manoeuvre afforded the rest of us an uninterrupted view of Linda's underwear, which consisted of plain white pants and flesh-coloured tights with a sturdily reinforced gusset. It must have occurred to us all simultaneously that if this evening Linda were to be struck down by the number 6 to Basset Regis she would have nothing whatever of which to be ashamed.

We also noted that Linda's legs were good right up to the top, were free of cellulite and broken veins, and had recently been subjected to the bikini wax which is the stamp of the well-organised woman.

I glanced at the others. Bernice, thank God, was reorganising her jacket to withstand the rigours of the game; Damon was tying his shoelaces; and Constantine was looking on with complete detachment over his glass of water. Linda's crotch, it appeared, held no interest for him. I dare say he saw too many in the course of his work.

To be fair to Linda, as Mike hoisted her about, hauling on her right arm and bending her left like a piston, elbow first, to the ground, she exhibited the most admirable British *sang-froid*, such as enabled many a spunky Victorian lady to travel through uncharted mountain wastes 'With Mule and Notebook'.

'All right down there?' asked Mike.

'As well as can be expected.'

'Ready, timer?' Constantine nodded, waving his left wrist. 'We're off?' They moved off, soixante-neufing it down the hall (Mike having negotiated the narrow doorway with consummate skill) like some elaborate monster from the mists of mythology.

We fell about. We all thought each other so perfectly splendid, so amusing and attractive (this with the possible exception of Damon) that it would have taken a disaster of cataclysmic proportions to shake our convivial mood. That disaster was coming, we could not know how soon, but for now, like the sun-kissed hedonists of that long Edwardian summer, we continued to laugh like drains.

The Channings, as befitted the experts, completed their circuit in a nippy thirty-two seconds, without mishap. Linda regained the vertical with more dignity than she had a right to, her well-cut coiffure falling back into place at once and her colour returning to normal in less than a minute.

'Thirty-two seconds to beat!' cried Mike. 'Right, Bernice, you ready?'

'Sir!'

'You?' Mike looked at Damon.

'Guess so.' I had to admire Damon's calm – his 'cool' I suppose he would have called it – and could only suppose it masked a kind of inertia panic. The situation in which he found himself was so totally foreign to him that his stunted verbal and·facial vocabulary had not the wherewithal to express an appropriate reaction.

Mike drew a piece of paper from the vase. In the declamatory tones of a fairground barker he called out: 'Buttocks! Buttocks are trumps!'

'Buttocks, schmuttocks,' said Bernice airily. 'Sit down, Damon.'

Damon sat.

'Take your shoes off,' Bernice instructed, 'and lock your ankles round my upper thighs. Then we clasp wrists and ankles and Bob's your uncle!'

Damon had no uncle Bob. He was a hopelessly inept pupil. Perhaps his ghastly assumed phlegm had meant suppressing his powers of rational thought – never all that great – as well. Also, as his work for me had indicated, he was assiduous but cack-handed. It took a full three minutes for Bernice to get a grip on him, and he on the situation, and they subsequently failed to complete the course.

Bernice and Damon locked together looked like one of the unlikelier illustrations from the *Karma Sutra*. His day-glo socks sprouting from beneath her ample bottom, her black belt tickling his ever-reddening nose, encapsulated exactly what is meant by the term culture clash. His peg was square and her hole round, and even had there been the remotest possibility of the one coming into contact with the other, no conjunction would have been possible.

'Let me get you a drink, Damon,' I said, as he staggered stiffly in from the hall, where Bernice had summarily dumped him.

He croaked something affirmative and I fetched him a can of Pils from the fridge. He sat on the sofa, staring glazedly in front of him, nursing the can on his chest and taking occasional gulps from it. I didn't like the look of him. It was hard to imagine what it was like for a culturally deprived seventeen-year-old of limited experience to be carried upside down by a woman of Bernice's build and background at a dinner party of his employer's.

'Our turn, I believe,' said Constantine. He placed his hand on my shoulder and left it there. In any man not so patently a gentleman it would have been a frankly flirtatious gesture. I wondered if I felt hot and sweaty through the purple silk.

Mike put his hand in the vase and drew out a bit of paper.

'It's a real bugger!' he cried. 'Right knee!'

'Perhaps,' I said sportingly, 'I'd better take my tights off.'

'I know,' said Constantine. 'You put your left foot in my trouser pocket.'

'Steady on,' intervened Mike. 'Not allowed. All perks must be incidental. Feet in pockets are out.'

Bernice and Linda cackled with laughter. Damon sank still lower on the sofa, the can of Pils almost obscuring his face.

'Very well,' said Constantine. 'Back to the drawing board.'

In the end we solved the problem by these means: Constantine laced his fingers behind my back, and I draped my left leg over his arm; I bent my right leg so that the knee brushed the ground, and he grabbed my foot with his fingers and held it up. I had not been in such acute discomfort since I'd played Long John Silver at boarding school, but I was heedless of it. Anaesthetised by lust I dangled there, my face bobbing not six inches from Constantine's fly, his tantalising scent in my nostrils, the pre-shrunk denim which covered his narrow hips brushing from time to time my fiery cheek.

'Ready?' asked Mike. 'Then go!'

With the cheers of the onlookers ringing in our ears we set off. It was a kind of torture by proximity. The more exhausted we both became, the tighter I had to clasp Constantine's belt at the back, and the more firmly my face was pressed against him. It would have taken only the slightest reciprocal pressure, the merest twitch, the smallest suggestion of engorgement, and I should have cast caution and sportsmanship to the winds and wrestled my partner to the ground. But as we bumped and dragged along the hall like a murderer and his victim no one would have guessed at these salacious fantasies.

By the time we turned at the front door – where Mike, acting as invigilator, bounded round us, studying our technique – my joints were screaming in agony, but this was as nothing beside my agonies of frustration. I reflected that this might well turn out to be the closest I ever came to unveiling the secrets of Constantine's inner leg, for this ludicrous parody would probably put him off for good.

'You won! Twenty-eight seconds! You won, you jammy buggers!' cried Bernice, as we hurtled with a final turn of speed back into the sitting room.

Then several things happened simultaneously. We collapsed on the floor, still locked in our position, my face now entirely smothered by Constantine's crotch; the uncurtained windows were suddenly piled with staring faces, mostly young, male, and wearing expressions of astonished glee; and Damon was extravagantly sick.

For a brief, half-stifled moment I twisted my head and rolled my eyes and took it all in. Then I closed my eyes once more and concentrated desperately on what was surely going to be my first and final clinch with the Greek doctor.

Astonishing how quickly the euphoric effects of alcohol and lively social intercourse are dispelled by embarrassment. From a tableau which in its peculiar nastiness must have resembled a sort of white-collar gang-bang (or, given my position, gang-blow), we resumed our separate and relatively respectable identities with lightning speed. Constantine ministered to the gagging Damon (whose indisposition, it was all too luridly apparent, was attributable to the merging of pork scratchings, rum and coke, and ice-cold Pils); Bernice flew to the kitchen for detergent and cloth; Mike Channing changed the tape; and Linda poured cold coffee with a trembling hand. An imperious knock sounded on the front door, and the wall of grinning faces moved away from the window. I stuffed my tights behind the sofa cushion, slipped on my shoes and marched, with grim robotic calm, into the hall.

On the doorstep were as unwelcome a group as in my wildest nightmares I could have envisaged. At the head of a tight phalanx of smirking lads in green shirts – the 2nd Basset Scout Troop – stood Glynis Makepeace, clad in the armour of light: badges, belt, beret, lanyard, whistle and woggle. Just behind her was Nita Nutkin in a broderie anglaise peasant blouse and red gingham pinafore. The contrast between the two was startling, but for one thing – they wore identical expressions of tight-lipped disapproval.

'Well, hallo!' I squeaked. 'Hallo, Gareth!'

'It's unfortunate,' said Akela, and I knew she considered the misfortune to be entirely hers, 'that we have to disturb you when you've got company.'

'Not at all.'

'We have a problem,' she boomed, calling the meeting to order. 'Baloo has come to grief.'

A nervous tic fluttered in my right cheek. 'Good heavens.'

'He's at our house, the poor thing,' chittered Nita, getting in on the act. 'Stan's got him on the sofa right now.'

'I suspect it's nothing but a wrench,' said Glynis in an accusatory tone. God help Baloo if he was found to be malingering. 'We've taken all the usual first-aid precautions, but it had best be looked at.'

'Probably.' I was beginning to get their drift.

Glynis's eyes swivelled alarmingly as she watched Bernice nip across behind me on her second journey to the sink with the bucket and the bottle of Kleeneze.

'I believe,' said Glynis, 'you have the doctor here? Dr Kikarse?' She enunciated a version of Constantine's name with elaborate distaste.

This had to be a rhetorical question, since only minutes before she had seen Constantine and me intertwined in a kind of human sheep-shank on the sitting room floor.

'We rang the surgery exchange from my house,' explained Nita, 'and they gave this number for the doctor on call, and your Gareth said – '

'Yes, yes.' Murderously, I scanned the faceless horde of scouts for my son. 'The doctor is here. Why don't you come in for a moment?'

They surged past. Akela, disfavour made flesh; Nita, bright-eyed and curious, hoping no doubt to stumble on a sparsely clad gigolo snorting cocaine from an apostle spoon; the scouts, all agog for a fresh glimpse of the sink of depravity which was my home; and after them a dozen or so tiny cubs who (I prayed) must have been far too short to see anything through the sitting room window.

'If Dr Kikarse can spare a minute,' said Akela, 'Anita can escort him back to her house, and I will accompany the troop to my garden for refreshments. 'My husband,' she added, 'has gone on to start a fire.'

'Has he?' I said. 'Just hang on for a second, will you?'

I went back to the sitting room and closed the door behind me. My guests, and Damon, had assumed a sort of studied casualness which would have fooled no one. The twin stenches of semi-digested alcohol and Kleeneze had combined to produce an atmosphere like one of the larger London Gents.

Each clasped a cup of cold coffee and they were listening to Tom Lehrer. The screeches of appreciative laughter emanating from the sound centre contrasted sharply with their expressions of introspective gloom.

'What's up?' enquired Mike, perking up no end at my arrival. 'Anything we can do?'

'Not really. Constantine, it's you they want.'

'What? Me?' He stood up with indecent haste. 'Who?'

'There's a patient for you at the Atkins' House,' I said.

'What, another? Mr and Mrs Atkins? I was there last Saturday too.'

'It's not actually them – '

'No, it wasn't last time,' he explained enthusiastically, 'it was one of their guests. Got tangled in a lariat, and in struggling to free himself knocked over a pot of hot barbecue beans all down his legs. Fortunately he was wearing – '

'They're waiting for you in the hall,' I said. 'Rebecca of Sunnybrook Farm, and Akela.'

'I'm coming. By the way,' he added on the way out, 'I don't know how Damon got here this evening, but he certainly shouldn't be in charge of anything on wheels.'

'Oh, I'll run my partner home,' volunteered Bernice, slapping the whey-faced Damon on the knee. 'One lift's much like another, eh Damon?'

He moaned weakly.

Out in the hall Constantine was all practised solicitude.

'We meet again, Mrs Atkins. How is Mr Hickrock?'

'Oh fine, absolutely fine – we must stop meeting like this!'

'Absolutely. Now what's the trouble this time?'

Akela stepped forward. 'My Baloo has incurred a wrench.'

For a moment I could see Constantine mentally riffling through a hundred medical textbooks. 'Sorry?'

'One of the cub leaders,' explained Nita. 'His ankle.'

'Take me to him, Mrs Atkins,' said Constantine. Then Nita bore him, his bedside manner and his little black bag off into the night.

'Work of moments,' said Akela scornfully. The cubs and scouts had retired into the kitchen, and now she flung open the door to reveal them pre-empting the bangers and dampers with bowls of cereal.

'Troop – out!' she commanded, and they obeyed like lambs, adding at least ten bowls and spoons to the existing washing up.

'Troop – to Jubilee Close – forward!' rapped Akela. I watched with grudging admiration as the 2nd Bassets shuffled off. She certainly had the problem of discipline licked. I wondered if a tie and forage cap would help me, but concluded that without Glynis's many natural advantages I should simply appear ludicrous.

I closed the door after them, and leaned on it for a second, a broken woman, before going back to the others.

It was eleven o'clock and my beautiful, well-planned dinner party now resembled nothing so much as a brisk evening at Vine Street Police Station – an uneasy melange of drunks, casualties, loose women and under-age offenders. And to top it all Constantine had been taken from me, carried away on a tide of malign circumstances against which it had been bootless to struggle.

Someone had replaced Tom Lehrer with Clara's Badness album, the monotonous, sardonic flavour of which was perfectly suitable for the terminal stages of a disastrous social occasion.

Bernice leapt to her feet, chest aquiver.

'Right, I'm off! Damon, on your feet, your carriage awaits.'

'Bernice!' I wailed. 'Don't go – I need you!'

'No you don't!' she replied. 'Damon needs his kip a lot more, don't you, Damon?'

Damon responded with a damp, wavering snore. Bernice hauled him to his feet.

'Where does he live?'

'Scargill Cuttings, Basset Regis. You'll have to ask him the number. I say Bernice, are you sure – '

'Sure as eggs. Thank you, my dear,' she kissed my cheek, supporting Damon on one arm, 'for a gorgeous dinner. I shall be on the blower anon.'

I saw them out, and watched them go, listing and tottering like a couple of amateur caber-throwers, through my front gate.

Mike and Linda Channing had taken on the appearance of

fixtures and fittings, blending in to the background to see what might transpire.

I sank down in a chair with a groan.

'Jolly enjoyable evening,' said Mike. 'Plenty to drink, bit of rough trade – ' I supposed he meant Bernice and Damon – 'raided by scouts, next best thing to being raided by the Bill. Pity you've lost old Kildare, though.'

'Yes.' It was a pity all right. I'd almost certainly scared off the one person I wished to attract, and prematurely ruined my reputation in the process. Vividly I recalled Nita Nutkin's smug, beady-eyed curiosity, and Akela's formidable disapprobation as she shielded her tender charges from contamination.

'I think I'll shoot myself,' I said.

'Oh, don't do that,' said Linda. And added 'How's George?', thus producing like a rabbit from a hat the one remaining topic guaranteed to speed my decline.

'Don't ask her that,' said Mike, leaning over and poking his wife in the ribs. 'She might tell you.'

'What about the book?' went on Linda, displaying the impervious tenacity which was such an asset in her work. 'How's that coming along?'

'Slowly and painfully.'

'If you want my opinion,' said Linda, 'which I'm sure you don't, I think you're due for a shake-up. A change of tack. A whole new thing.' And as if she hadn't mouthed enough banalities for one evening she added: 'I reckon there's a different Harriet in there somewhere, just struggling to get out!'

I finally burst into shrill, hysterical laughter.

My Day: An
Introduction of
Sorts

◆

Fran Lebowitz

12:35 P.M. – The phone rings. I am not amused. This is not my favorite way to wake up. My favorite way to wake up is to have a certain French movie star whisper to me softly at two-thirty in the afternoon that if I want to get to Sweden in time to pick up my Nobel Prize for Literature I had better ring for breakfast. This occurs rather less often than one might wish.

Today is a perfect example, for my caller is an agent from Los Angeles who informs me that I don't know him. True, and not without reason. He is audibly tan. He is interested in my work. His interest has led him to the conclusion that it would be a good idea for me to write a movie comedy. I would, of course, have total artistic freedom, for evidently comic writers have taken over the movie business. I look around my apartment (a feat readily accomplished by simply glancing up) and remark that Dino De Laurentiis would be surprised to hear that. He chuckles tanly and suggests that we talk. I suggest that we *are* talking. He, however, means *there* and at my own expense. I reply that the only way I could get to Los Angeles at my own expense is if I were to go by postcard. He chuckles again and suggests that we talk. I agree to talk just as soon as I have won the Nobel Prize – for outstanding achievement in physics.

12:55 P.M. – I try to get back to sleep. Although sleeping is an area in which I have manifested an almost Algeresque grit and persistence, I fail to attain my goal.

1:20 P.M. – I go downstairs to get the mail. I get back into bed. Nine press releases, four screening notices, two bills, an invitation to a party in honor of a celebrated heroin addict, a final disconnect notice from New York Telephone, and three hate letters from *Mademoiselle* readers demanding to know just what it is that makes me think that I have the right to regard houseplants – *green, living* things – with such marked distaste. I call the phone company and try to make a deal, as actual payment is not a possibility. Would they like to go to a screening? Would they care to attend a party for a heroin addict? Are they interested in knowing just what it is that makes me think that I have the right to regard houseplants with such marked distaste? It seems they would not. They would like $148.10. I agree that this is, indeed, an understandable preference, but caution them against the bloodless quality of a life devoted to the blind pursuit of money. We are unable to reach a settlement. I pull up the covers and the phone rings. I spend the next few hours fending off editors, chatting amiably, and plotting revenge. I read. I smoke. The clock, unfortunately, catches my eye.

3:40 P.M. – I consider getting out of bed. I reject the notion as being unduly vigorous. I read and smoke a bit more.

4:15 P.M. – I get up feeling curiously unrefreshed. I open the refrigerator. I decide against the half a lemon and jar of Gulden's mustard and on the spur of the moment choose instead to have breakfast out. I guess that's just the kind of girl I am – whimsical.

5:10 P.M. – I return to my apartment laden with magazines and spend the remainder of the afternoon reading articles by writers who, regrettably, met their deadlines.

6:55 P.M. – A romantic interlude. The object of my affections arrives bearing a houseplant.

9:30 P.M. – I go to dinner with a group of people that includes two fashion models, a fashion photographer, a fashion photographer's representative, and an art director. I occupy myself almost entirely with the art director – drawn to him largely because he knows the most words.

2:05 A.M. – I enter my apartment and prepare to work. In deference to the slight chill I don two sweaters and an extra pair of socks. I pour myself a club soda and move the lamp next to the desk. I reread several old issues of *Rona Barrett's Hollywood* and a fair piece of *The Letters of Oscar Wilde*. I pick up my pen and stare at the paper. I light a cigarette. I stare at the paper. I write, *My Day: An Introduction of Sorts*. Good. Lean yet cadenced. I consider my day. I become unaccountably depressed. I doodle in the margin. I jot down an idea I have for an all-black version of a Shakespearean comedy to be called *As You Likes It*. I look longingly at my sofa, not unmindful of the fact that it converts cleverly into a bed. I light a cigarette. I stare at the paper.

4:50 A.M. – The sofa wins. Another victory for furniture.

THE TROUBLE WITH A PERFECT LOVER...

Sybylla de Montagna

◆

Did your mother ever tell you sex is a real can of worms? Mine did. And, sad to say, experience tends to bear her out. Which is why it gives me great pleasure to announce – no – proclaim – that I am fortunate enough to have the most considerate, aware lover in the world. I don't want to encourage the lewd or salacious, so I'll just say: 'No one I have ever met hits the spot (so to speak) quite as well.'

But sex with yourself – it's a little lonely sometimes, isn't it?

I'll tell you what I miss. Apart from the laugh afterwards (you know, he says: 'How was it for you?' You say: 'What can I tell you – it was the best two minutes of my life.' He says: 'Come again?' You: Laugh) – apart from that there's really one thing missing: goosepimples.

I can't give myself goosepimples because I always know what I'm going to do next.

Loosen up, I tell myself. Go with the flow. But I always know which flow I'll go with.

I've tried surprising myself. Coming home early from work. Varying the position. Do you know how long it took me to get the knack of jumping myself from behind? I've tried doing it in unusual places – like Marks & Spencer's or the tube – you just get funny looks.

When you get right down to it – and I am telling you, I

have – there is nothing I can do that gets me biting lumps from the mattress. The only thing that makes me gargle is TCP. Why are there no sex aids that nibble the back of your neck?

Still, it's got to be Safe Sex. I can be absolutely positive I won't get myself a dose of something nasty. No worries there. Think about it: it means you won't suffer terribly, become a shadow of your former self and die miserably – like when you get married. It's so easy – there are no demands. You never give yourself a hard time. You never sulk because you don't feel like it.

I take myself out to dinner now and then. Bring myself tea in bed. I buy myself flowers. Little surprises. I've always got time to really listen to me. What more can a woman ask for? Anyway, you will have to excuse me, I have to go now and whisper something in my ear.

MADAM AND THE MINI-BAR

Libby Purves

$\blacklozenge$

Every now and then – with shrinking reluctance, with shame and modest loathings – one is forced to admit that it is, after all, possible that women are mad. It takes a lot to make me fall short of sisterhood in this distressing way: after all, I, too, have marched with a torch to Reclaim The Night in my time, chanting *Whatever we wear, wherever we go, Yes means Yes and No means No.*

I have breast-fed infants on business flights while bankers glared coldly across their own lap-portable paraphernalia (equally intrusive. Mine, after all, only slurped quietly. Theirs bleeped loudly). I have defended the weird workings of the GLC Women's Committee to the last gallant ditch at tweedy country dinner-parties; I have broken in righteously to re-prove John Timpson, on the air, for ho-ho-ing about boys having to do needlework in school. (Actually, that particular one backfired: the crafty bastard was only looking for a feed-line in order to brag that he was rather good at embroidery.) But anyway, in my modest way I have always steamed down the line with the feminist flag flying.

Until I hit the buffers, two weeks ago. *Crash.* I opened the paper to find myself required to start worrying about women in hotels. Not, you understand, about how the hell a homeless bed-and-breakfast family with three toddlers is supposed to survive for years in one small room in a King's Cross flophouse. No: this item was on someone's report about another aspect of hotel horror: the 'problems' of lone women who travel on business.

The situation, it appears, is grim. Women 'cannot drink alone in a hotel bar without being accosted'. They are treated off-handedly in hotel dining-rooms and therefore (*gasp*) 'condemned to Room Service'. Hotels are designed predominantly for business men, not women; and what is required is a 'Charter of Rights' for women travellers, including specially labelled tables set aside in the dining-room so that they can find other wincing females and all huddle together like wildebeest at a drinking-hole, safe from the prowling lion and mocking jackal.

Now if I had never been to a hotel on my own, but only on some protective manly arm, I might conceivably have been swayed to indignation by all this. One might picture violent sexual passes in the foyer, leering waiters exposing themselves over the soup, and terrified women crouching in their rooms afraid to telephone for a toasted-cheese sandwich and a Diet Pepsi (£14.50 excluding service), in case the operator should loose off a torrent of jeering abuse about their inability to get a Man to travel with them.

But as it happens I have lived through many a weary night alone in British hotels: in my radio reporting days, the management used to get periodic fits of guilt about being too London-centred, and pick on some poor devil to go and 'beat up a region'. You weren't allowed back without at least six features: so once you'd mopped up the Wisbech floods and filed three minutes fifty seconds of whimsy about the Spalding Flower Festival, you were left flailing desperately around in the local *Herald and Argus* for enough borough council scandals and singing ferrets to make up your quota. Add to that the Royal Visits, Party Conferences, and assorted gritty documentaries on the troubles of washing-machine factories, and you have a goodly number of solitary nights spent in business hotels, staring at the Mini-Bar and wondering

whether the expenses claim could stand another quick miniature of Jack Daniels.

I have done all this, yet cannot espouse the new crusade;
just can't see it, somehow. Too insensitive to waiters' insults,
perhaps, too butch, too scruffily dressed to invite passes?
Whatever the reason, my feet fail to twitch to the new
drum-beat.

The trouble is that nobody with any sense who had ever
stayed in a British business-persons' hotel would claim that
such establishments are 'designed predominantly for men'. In
fact, they are not intended for human beings at all. They are
designed to accommodate gigantic Conferences, to look lux-
urious in group brochure photographs, and for the further-
ance of the scientific study of portion control and Carvery
salad-display design. Hotels are not places fit for free men and
women, born to walk upright in the sunlight, any more than
zoos are suitable for cheetahs.

The most chilling newspaper photograph of the month was
of those poor little Dewsbury children in the education dis-
pute being given lessons in 'a function room' in a local hotel.
The sight of those innocent, clean little faces in front of the
dark, debased gothick flock wallpaper and beneath the sleazy,
murky wall-bracket lamps was truly horrible. You could
almost *smell* last night's *Coq au vin* and *Pommes Duchesse*.
Only cockroaches and Rotarians should be asked to dwell in
such dark places.

So you see it is not just women: there has never been a
person born who could feel truly comfortable in a British
business hotel. Those waiters are not sneering at you, madam,
with any particular venom: they sneer at everyone, because
they are so bored and because the chemical fumes rising off
the long-life coleslaw buffet have slightly unhinged their poor
minds. That sinister sound you hear outside your room is not
a sexist voyeur sawing a peephole to look at your Janet
Regers: it is a sad and disoriented sales rep who misses his kids
just as much as you do, trying to fit his key into the wrong

room door after six vodkatinis with a client whom he knows was only playing cat-and-mouse with him. If the said rep should later 'accost' you in the bar on your chaste velour banquette, do at least consider that he may want to show you photographs of his dog, his baby, his loft conversion: accept him as a brother.

In any case, any woman senior enough to be sent off alone on a business trip with her hotel expenses paid is not worth her money if she can't repel a pass or two in a public place. This is not a Sex Harassment Horror situation, with some poor little sixteen-year-old YTS typist being goosed by a sweating great Boss-Man: this is a clash of equals, surely? Try saying, 'Get your hand off my knee, you dirty beast, I've got a Travel Scrabble set here ...' He'll probably be grateful. He might even know a lot of exciting new words, about valves and things.

Anyway, what on earth are you *doing* 'drinking alone in a hotel bar'? Have you no work to do? Is there nothing to see in this new city? Anyone, of any sex, who sits alone in a hotel bar for more than five minutes can be reasonably assumed to be in some way desperate: perhaps the chap accosting you is a Samaritan touting for business? Besides, I cannot muster sympathy for self-inflicted wounds: you've probably got the clothes wrong.

In the good old days, business women and the secretaries of businessmen dressed properly in acres of practical grey serge, with their hair in a bun so that Mr Right could one day unpin it and say, 'Miss Jones, you're beautiful!' Mr Wrong, on the other hand, could merely give her a dismissive flicker of the eyes, and pass on to something peroxide with its skirt hitched high on a barstool. Simple. These days, corporate female executives feel it incumbent upon them to dress like the grasping trollops in *Dynasty*, and wear silk stockings and lip-gloss for boardroom credibility. You can't blame an old-fashioned chap who is as thick as a brick, slightly drunk, and utterly miserable (due to being in a British business hotel) if he gets confused and spots your blusher and the seams on your stockings before he notices your Filofax.

You're basically safe, anyway: he and you both know that one piercing shriek would instantly bring ten waiters and an agitated Conference Manager out of the oakette woodwork. Pull yourself together, woman! I shall not be marching at your side. Reclaiming the Night was worth the bother. Reclaiming the Grill Room isn't.

THE RIGHT
APPROACH

— ◆ —

Alice Thomas Ellis

Sometimes Beryl laughs so much she has to lie down. She did the other day. We were in our local trying to have a talk without disturbance – something impossible in the home – and a foreign gentleman apparently mistook me for a lady of the night. I can't imagine why. I was wearing my ladylike grey flannel and had my hair scraped right back. Nonetheless he kept telling me that he had just 15 minutes and more or less insisting that I nip outside and help him to occupy them. I told him I was a married lady and very religious and he got quite indignant. He would tap himself on the chest saying he had all the love, and then he'd attempt to do the same thing to me, saying I had the experience. Sauce. It was at that point that Beryl had to lie down, sobbing with uncontrollable hysteria. I was trying to maintain a serious demeanour because I didn't particularly want to hurt the wretched man's feelings, and also these scenes can get quite tense if one is not careful. Fortunately the 15 minutes elapsed and he was required back at his place of work.

We took Jeff to Mass last Sunday, creeping into the pub beforehand for a fortifying vodka. What was my astonishment – for this is far from Jeff's manor – to hear a voice saying 'Hi Jeff.' 'Hallo Boris,' responded Jeffrey with what seemed to me to be modified enthusiasm. Boris bought us all a drink and insisted on lending Jeff a fiver, so I said, as we departed.

'What a nice man', and Jeffrey agreed that he was charming but added that he had a nasty job.

'Oh poor thing,' we said sympathetically, 'what does he do?'

'He's a burglar,' said Jeff.

That's one of the things I like about this part of the world – you meet all sorts. Only last week I was trotting towards the station averting the eyes from the winos who stand or sit by the back wall of the cinema, a line of pee leading from each to the gutter, reminding one of the chickens and chalk lines, when a young man darted out of a doorway requesting the loan of a match. No point here in pretending not to have seen him, so we got into conversation. He had two companions – one utterly silent, and one a pretty girl. He said they were Irish travelling people and I didn't like to ask what that meant – gypsies, tinkers, or just Irish people who got about a lot? With the novelist's interest in raw material I enquired their names. He said reassuringly that he was known as Jerry the Street Fighter. So I hastily asked the name of the girl.

'Mary de Rothschild,' she responded.

'Pardon?' I said.

'Mary the Lost Child,' she repeated. That made me want to cry, so I departed the poorer by a match and a couple of quid. Jerry offered me a swig from his bottle and I said I was a teetotaller. He intimated that it might be nice if they all came home with me, and then he kissed me. I really must change my perfume. When I *think* of the strictures I put upon the daughter about not talking to strangers.

A couple of years ago I broke Rule Number One. I had been to see Caroline and instead of calling a cab to the house I went off to pick one up at Brompton Road. Unfortunately the pubs were just emptying and every time I hailed a taxi it was whipped away by pairs of very alarming men, some bold in black leather hung about with chains, and some with Mexican-type moustaches. I was not disposed to argue with them so I stood in the rain growing quietly desperate. After a while a private car drew up and a gentleman leaned out and asked if he could give me a lift. Before you could say 'rape' I had hopped in. Can you believe it? I realised immediately, of course, that I was a much more foolish person than I had previously supposed and began a very Cheltenham tea-table conversation about the weather and the cost of private education in my most modulated tones. He was a dear kind man up from the country for the day and he drove me straight home – some considerable distance – declining to come in and meet my husband and join us in a cup of coffee. I don't know what he must have thought. *No* well brought up woman gets into the cars of strange men. I was lucky there, but I have instructed my friends never to let me out alone after a convivial evening. I can't be trusted.

The nuns used to observe a ploy known as 'custody of the eyes' which sounds rather disgustingly culinary and reminds me of St Lucy. They don't do it any more since Vatican II, beaming out frankly at the world and exchanging greetings on the street, but I'm going to do it in future. I shall keep the gaze fixed on the middle distance, glancing neither to right nor left. I'll probably break my neck.

TOO LATE, TOO LATE, SO NEVER CALL ME MOTHER

♦

Lynne Truss

An old friend of mine, who five years ago migrated to the country with her husband to propagate children and rear a garden, recently sent me a card which I didn't know quite how to take. 'Wishing you all good luck', she wrote, 'on your chosen path.' I sat looking at it with my fingers in my mouth. What did she mean, exactly, by this notion of the 'chosen path'? I assumed she meant it kindly, but it made me feel suddenly exposed and distant. Hey, where did everybody go? Supposing that she imagined herself on a path radically divergent from mine, I instantly pictured myself labouring alone up a narrow, steep, dusty, brambly trail with a determined look on my face, as though illustrating a modern-day parable about the grim sacrifices of feminism.

So vivid was this picture, in fact, that I could feel the stinging nettles brushing against my legs. It was awful. I felt thirsty; my head swam; the sun scorched my shoulders. Looking down, I observed my friend ambling happily in the sunshine on a broad level path with a pram and husband, while small apple-cheeked children ran off to right and left, frolicking with lambs. I would have watched for longer, but a bloke called Bunyan came along and told me to hop it. Said I was straying on his territory. So luckily that was that.

But I was definitely confused by the notion of the chosen path, and dwelt on it for days. Did I *choose* this, then? And if

217

so, why couldn't I remember doing it? Hadn't I always thought, rather naïvely, that there was still time to make these decisions about wife-and-motherhood in the future – that the crossroads were just over the horizon? But it turns out that the last exit was miles back, and I am a person whose chosen path speaks for itself. The hardest part was realising I can never be a teenage tennis phenomenon. How on earth did I let things drift so badly?

For some reason I thought of the careers mistress at school – perhaps because she represents the single point in my life when I recognised a T-junction and made a definite choice. She wanted us all to be nurses, you see; and I refused. Brainy sixth-formers would queue at the careers office with fancy ideas about Oxford and Cambridge and archaeology, and come out again 15 seconds later, waving nursing application forms and looking baffled. 'You have to have A-levels to be a nurse now, you know, Miss Hoity-Toity!' she would bark after them, twitching. And then, turning to the next in line, 'Now, my dear, which branch of the noble profession do *you* want to join?'

At my age, women are supposed to hear the loud ticking of a biological clock, but I think I must have bought the wrong battery for mine. The only time I experienced the classic symptoms was when I desperately wanted a car. It was weird. If I spotted another woman driving a Peugeot 205, I would burst into tears. In the end, friends tactfully stopped mentioning their cars in my presence ('My Volvo did *such* a funny thing the other day – oh Lynne, how awful, I didn't see you'). And there was that one shameful occasion when I lurked outside a supermarket half-considering snatching a Metro. 'What a lovely bonnet you've got,' I whispered, fingering it lightly. But then a woman shouted 'Oi!', so I picked up my string bag and scarpered.

Now I realise that what I want is a book. So much do I want to give birth to a book that I experience 'false alarms' – where I think I am 'with book', but am not really. Once a month I phone up my agent and say 'It's happening!' And she says, 'How marvellous!' And then I have to ring again a week later and say 'Bad news,' and she says, 'Never mind, conception is a mysterious thing.' I suddenly realise that a book would be a comfort in my old age, and I try to ignore the argument that there are already too many books in the world competing for the available shelf-space. Mine, of course, will be a poor fatherless mite, but I shall love it all the more for that.

Perhaps the image of the paths and crossroads is just the wrong one. Perhaps I did always know where I wanted to go, but just walked backwards with my eyes closed, pretending there was no act of will involved. Because I do recall from early youth that while other children pleaded with their mums for miniature bridal outfits and little dolls that went wee-wees, I was campaigning for a brick-built Wendy House in the garden where I could lock the door and sit at an enormous typewriter. My only imaginary friends were phantom insurance collectors, a man from Porlock and the printer's boy.

My idea of a Wendy House was a rather grandiose one, I suppose. It involved guttering and utilities and a mantelpiece where I could put the rent money, not to mention trouble with the drains. I remember when a little friend told me she had acquired a Wendy House, and I was wild with envy. But, when I went to see it, it was just a canvas job with painted-on windows. Fancy telling a gullible kid that this was a Wendy House. Sometimes I wonder what happened when she eventually uncovered the deception. Probably she married somebody with a big house and had lots of kids in double-quick time, to establish a sense of security. In which case, I wish her all good luck on her chosen path.

Hip Wedding on
Mount Tam

♦

Cyra McFadden

As she got ready for Martha's wedding, Kate reflected happily that one great thing about living in Marin was that your friends were always growing and changing. She couldn't remember, for example, how many times Martha had been married before.

She wondered if she ought to call her friend Carol and ask what to wear. Martha had said 'dress down,' but that could mean anything from Marie Antoinette milkmaid from The Electric Poppy to bias-cut denims from Moody Blues. Kate didn't have any bias-cut denims, because she'd been waiting to see how long they'd stay in, but she could borrow her adolescent daughter's. They wore the same clothes all the time.

Her husband, Harvey, was already in the shower, so Kate decided on her Renaissance Faire costume. She always felt mildly ridiculous in it, but it wasn't so bad without the conical hat and it was definitely Mount Tam wedding. Now the problem was Harvey, who absolutely refused to go to Mount Tam weddings in the French jeans Kate had bought him for his birthday. She knew he'd wear his Pierre Cardin suit, which was fine two years ago but which was now establishment; and, when he came out of the shower, her fears were confirmed.

Since they were already late, though, there was no point in trying to do something about Harvey. They drove up Panoramic to the mountain meadow trying to remember what

Martha's bridegroom's name was this time (Harvey thought it was Bill again, but Kate was reasonably sure it wasn't) and made it to the ceremony just as the recorder player, a bare-chested young man perched faunlike on a rock above the assembled guests, began to improvise variations on the latest Pink Floyd.

Right away, Kate spotted Carol and knew her Renaissance dress was all right – marginal, but all right. Carol was wearing Marie Antoinette milkmaid, but with her usual infallible chic, had embellished it with her trademark jewelry: an authentic squash-blossom necklace, three free-form rings bought from a creative artisan at the Mill Valley Art Festival on her right hand, and her old high school charm bracelet updated with the addition of a tiny silver coke spoon.

Reverend Spike Thurston, minister of the Radical Unitarian Church in Terra Linda and active in the Marin Sexual Freedom League, was presiding. Kate was thrilled as the ceremony began and Thurston raised a solemn, liturgical hand; she really got off on weddings.

'Fellow beings,' Thurston began, smiling, 'I'm not here today as a minister but as a member of the community. Not just the community of souls gathered here, not just the community of Mill Valley, but the larger human community which is the cosmos.

'I'm not going to solemnize this marriage in the usual sense of the word. I'm not going to pronounce it as existing from this day forward. Because nobody can do that except Martha and' – he held a quick, worried conference with somebody behind him – 'and Bill.'

Harvey was already restless. 'Do we have to go to a reception after this thing?' he asked too loudly.

'Organic,' Kate whispered, digging her fingernails into his wrist. 'At Davood's.'

Harvey looked dismayed.

'These children have decided to recite their own vows,' Thurston continued. Kate thought 'children' was overdoing it a little; Martha was at least forty, although everybody knew chronological age didn't matter these days. 'They're not going to recite something after me, because this is a *real* wedding – the wedding of two separatenesses, two solitarinesses, under the sky.'

Thurston pointed out the sky and paused while a jet thundered across it. Kate thought he looked incredibly handsome with his head thrown back and his purple Marvin Gaye T-shirt emblazoned with 'Let's Get It On' stretched tightly across his chest.

'Martha,' he said, 'will you tell us what's in your heart?'

Standing on tiptoe, Kate could just catch a glimpse of the bride; slightly to the right of her, she spotted Martha's ex-husband-once-removed with his spacy new old lady, who, Kate thought, looked like Martha. She tried to remember which of Martha's children, all present and looking oddly androgynous in velvet Lord Fauntleroy suits, were also his.

Martha recited a passage on marriage 'from the Spanish poet Federico García Lorca.' Last time she was married, she'd said, 'Frederico.' Kate thought the fact that Martha had got it right this time was a good sign; and she adored the Lorca.

When Bill recited in turn, he was almost inaudible, but Kate thought she recognized *The Prophet*, which was *not* a good sign. She dug her fingernails into Harvey again; he was shifting his feet restlessly. This wasn't a sign of anything, necessarily, since Harvey simply couldn't get used to his new Roots, but it was best to be safe.

'Hey, listen,' she whispered to Carol, who had wiggled her way through the crowd and was now at her side. 'It's terrific, isn't it?'

'Really,' Carol whispered back. 'He looks good. He's an architect that does mini-parks. She met him at her creative divorce group.'

Kate leaned across her to take in the crowd. She thought she recognized Mimi Fariña. She also noticed Larry, her shampoo person from Rape of the Locks, who always ran her through the soul handshake when she came in for a cut and blow-dry. She hoped she wouldn't have to shake hands with Larry at the reception, since she never got the scissors/paper/rock maneuvers of the soul handshake just right and since she was pretty sure that Larry kept changing it on her, probably out of repressed racial animosity.

Thurston, after a few remarks about the ecology, had just pronounced Martha and her new husband man and woman. Kate felt warmly sentimental as the bride and bridegroom kissed passionately, and loosened her grip on Harvey's wrist. She noticed that the fog was beginning to lift slightly and gazed off into the distance.

'Hey, look,' she said to Harvey excitedly. 'Isn't that the ocean?'

'The Pacific,' Harvey replied tersely. 'Believed to be the largest on the West Coast. It's part of the cosmos.'

Kate felt put down. Harvey was becoming increasingly uptight these days, and remarks like this one were more frequent. Look at the way he'd baited her TA instructor at the Brennans' the other night. 'You are not O.K.,' he had told him loudly, lurching slightly in his Roots. 'I could give you a lot of reasons; but take my word for it – you are *not* O.K.'

Yes, Kate was going to have to do something about Harvey...

A VISIT TO THE VET'S

A week later, Kate was still brooding over her husband Harvey's inscrutable behavior at Martha's wedding reception, where he had managed to offend just about everybody.

Harvey had turned down both the lentil loaf and the hash that was going around the room with a flat pronouncement that hash was illegal and lentil loaf ought to be. He had told several people who asked that his sign was the Mill Valley–East Blithedale turnoff. Finally, he had split entirely for an hour, only to reappear muttering darkly that the Old Mill Tavern had turned into 'some kind of goddamn fern bar.'

Kate wished that her friend Carol would finish doing Harvey's chart, for while some of his recent aberrations were typically Scorpio and therefore not his fault, she was beginning to suspect he had something weird she didn't know about on the cusp.

Just last night, for instance, over her favorite cassoulet out of 'Julia 2,' Kate had mentioned casually that she was interested in primal screaming and that she also thought she'd like to get rolfed. Harvey had said he figured if she got rolfed hard enough, she'd scream primally; he had then laughed so hard at his own feeble wit that he'd choked on his *saucisson*. Nobody could call Kate humorless. She never missed *Doonesbury* or *The Now People* and prized her 'Marcel Proust Was a Yenta' button. But she couldn't relate to Harvey's idea of what was funny these days. *No way*.

Her first impulse was to talk things over with her women's group, but the sisters weren't invariably as supportive as she'd hoped they'd be. Kate was still dealing with their reaction a few weeks ago when she'd mentioned that she'd like to take assertiveness training but was afraid Harvey wouldn't let her.

She was on her way to the Redwoode Veterinary Hospital, where she was going to leave her Manx, Kat Vonnegut, Jr, for a flea bath, when it suddenly occurred to her that maybe the answer to her dissatisfactions with Harvey was to get it on with somebody else. She just flashed on it: for once in her life, she ought to put her own needs right up front and then get behind them.

She parked out in back of the Redwoode, where the vets

hid their Mercedes 230 SL's, and extricated Kat Vonnegut, thumping around truculently in his cat carrier, from the rear of her VW bus. The hospital was expensive – it cost more to walk through the front door than it did for an office call to their family physician – but Kate was loyal to it because Dr Gelt had been so terrifically nice to her during Felix Frankfurter's final illness.

Not only had he encouraged her to come down and say goodbye to Felix just before he underwent what the computerized bill later designated 'EUTH & DISP,' but he had also encouraged her warmly to 'have another cat right away,' pointing out wisely that they wouldn't want to raise their Afghan, Donald Barthelme, as an only animal.

Anyway, because Mill Valley still had that real small-town atmosphere, she always met a lot of friends in the waiting room. First Peter, who taught a very popular course in 'Participatory Salad Making' at Heliotrope, appeared with his Irish setter. Peter had brought Panama Red in for a checkup because when he'd put his mood ring on the dog, just for a joke, it had turned black.

Then Julie, a former neighbor who had made it and moved up to Eldridge, came in to pick up Fanne Foxe Terrier, who had recently been raped, Julie explained, by a dachshund on a macho trip.

Julie had been the only other woman on the block who was heavily into macramé, and Kate missed her and the raps they'd had on lazy summer afternoons while they sat out on Julie's patio trying knots in plant hangers. She told Julie how she felt that life in a technocracy interfered with interpersonal relationships, and Julie agreed. 'For sure,' she said forcefully. 'Do you know how busy I've been lately? I haven't even read the last three issues of *Harper's. That's* how busy I've been.'

Eventually the orderly came to get Kat Vonnegut, and Kate went about her rounds. She stopped at Phillips for some Chemex filters and her own special blend of Madagascar, Senegalese and caffeine-free French roast, picked up a copy of

Zen and the Art of Motorcycle Maintenance for her eight-year-old nephew's birthday, and wound up at the Mill Valley Market, which was swarming with female tennis players.

You couldn't run around downtown Mill Valley in a bikini, which was tacky, but tennis dresses were socially acceptable anywhere. The tennis types tromped through the MVM in impeccable crotch-length whites, their deeply tanned legs flashing, little half moons of exposed white buttock glimmering as they leaned into the dairy cases for kefir, and the tassels that kept their socks up bobbing like cottontails at their heels. Kate, who hadn't signed up in time for membership in the Scott Valley Tennis Club, was deeply envious.

But her mind wasn't really on threads; she had definitely decided, maybe while she was buying WD-40 for Harvey's compost grinder at Varney's, to take a lover. Now the question was whose.

Just a few years ago, the husbands in her peer group had stroked her bare spine when she wore her backless black cocktail dress to parties and told her that she figured spectacularly in their dream lives. Now they were liberated; all the men she knew who had propositioned her had long since apologized and told her that they really, *really* respected her as a person. And of course she wouldn't be caught dead at a party anymore dressed as a sex symbol.

Poking kumquats and wondering if Harvey would eat jicama, Kate ran down the list of men she knew; they turned up rejects one after another, until she remembered Leonard. A psychologist specializing in the dysfunctional socialization of rich children, Leonard had an office in Tiburon, a reputation as a stud, and the warm, spontaneous personality of a true Sagittarius. He also had a lot of curly black chest hair which he displayed by wearing his shirts unbuttoned to the belly button.

Kate wasn't really high on chest hair because it seemed to collect devilled egg and little globs of hummus at stand-up

LETTERS FROM A FAINT-HEARTED FEMINIST

(AN EXTRACT)

◆

Jill Tweedie

21 January

Dear Mary,
Sorry I haven't written for a while, but back here in Persil Country the festive season lasts from November 1 (make plum pudding) to January 31 (lose hope and write husband's thank-you letters). I got some lovely presents. A useful Spare Rib Diary. A book called *The Implications of Urban Women's Image in Early American Literature*. A Marks and Sparks rape alarm. A canvas Backa-Pak so that the baby can come with me wherever I go – a sort of DIY rape alarm. And, of course, your bracing notelets, which will be boomeranging back to you for the rest of the year. Things I did not get for Christmas: a Janet Reger nightie, a feather boa, a pair of glittery tights.

Looking back, what with 'God Rest Ye Merry Gentlemen', 'Good King Wenceslas', 'Unto Us a Son is Born', 'We Three Kings', Father Christmas ho-hoing all over the place and the house full of tired and emotional males, I feel like I'm just tidying up after a marathon stag party. Our Lady popped up now and again but who remembers the words to *her* songs once they've left school? We learnt them but, then, ours was an all-girl school, in the business of turning out Virgin Mother replicas. If I ever get to heaven, I'll be stuck making manna in the Holy Kitchens and putti-sitting fat feathered babies quicker than I can say Saint Peter. Josh, on the other hand, will get a celestial club chair and a stiff drink. If God is a woman, why is She so short of thunderbolts?

I went to a fair number of parties dressed up as Wife of Josh but, to tell you the shameful truth, it was my Women's Collective beanfeast that finally broke my nerve. One wouldn't think one could work up a cold sweat about going as oneself to an all-woman party, would one? One can. I had six acute panic attacks about what to wear, for a start. Half my clothes are sackcloth, due to what Josh still calls my menopausal baby (come to me, my menopausal baby) and the other half are ashes, cold embers of the woman I once was. Fashion may well be a tool of women's oppression but having to guess is worse. In the end I went makeup-less in old flared jeans and saw, too late, that Liberation equals Calvin Klein and Lip Gloss or Swanky Modes and Toyah hair but not, repeat not, Conservative Association jumble. Misery brought on tunnel vision, I swooned like a Victorian lady and had to be woman-handled into a taxi home. Quelle fiasco.

That same evening, the blood back in my cheeks, I complained to Josh that I was cooking the three hundred and sixtieth meal of 1980 and he said move aside, I'll take over. Coming to, I found myself, family and carry-cot in a taxi driving to a posh restaurant. Very nice, too, but Josh was so smug afterwards that I felt it incumbent upon me, in the name of Wages for Housework, to point out that his solution to the domestic chore-sharing problem had just cost us fifty quid, and if he intended to keep that up, he'd have to apply for funding to the IMF. Bickered for the rest of the evening, Josh wittily intoning his Battle of Britain speech – you can please some of the women all of the time and all of the women ... but you know the rest, ha ha.

I had hardly recovered from these two blows to the system when Mother arrived to administer her weekly dose of alarm and despondency. How can I *think*, she said 18 times, of letting my Daughter drive van, alone, to Spain? Do I *want* her to be raped, mutilated and left for dead in foreign parts? It is my duty to insist that a *man* goes with her. I point out that Jane is a large, tough, twenty-year-old rather more competent than me. Mother and Mother's Husband put together and Mother leaves room in huff. I then had a panic attack about Jane being raped, mutilated and left for dead in foreign parts and insisted she took a man with her. Like the Yorkshire Ripper, you mean, shouted Jane and left room in huff.

Myself, I blame British Rail. Does Sir Peter Parker realize the mayhem caused to family units all over Britain by pound-a-trip Grans intent on injecting overdue guilt into long-unvisited daughters? Josh's Ma trained over, too, apparently to make sure I wouldn't grass on Josh if he turned out to be the Yorkshire Ripper. Ma, I said, what alternative would I have? Even the sacred marriage bonds might snap, given that one's spouse was a mass murderer. Marriage bonds maybe, she said, but I am his Mother. Then she said would I inform on Ben, I said what else could I do and she said you could stop his pocket money. She did. Ben, I said, glaring at the stick of celery that is my son, if I hear you've murdered one more woman, no sixpence for you next Friday. Well, now they've arrested someone who's got a wife and a mother. Keep your ears pinned back for the feminine connection.

Ben's friend Flanagan stayed most of the holiday. He explained that he had left home because his mother had this new boyfriend. How difficult it must be, I thought, for adolescent boys in the midst of the Oedipal Dilemma to have alien males vying for their love-object's favours. Flanagan said he couldn't stand the way his Mum bullied her boyfriends and now she had chucked them both out because of her women's meetings. You're as bad as the NFers, he told her. I can't help being a boy, can I, any more than if I was black? But you *are* black, Flanagan, I said, and Black is Beautiful. Yeah, except I'm white, he said. Flanagan's Dad is white, said Ben, so why shouldn't Flanagan choose? What am I, anyway, a racist or

AGAINST YOUTH

◆

Jilly Cooper

Two very pretty teenage girls with peace slogans across their bosoms rang my doorbell the other day. They made a terrible mistake, they said. Their friend was driving down from Clacton to meet them and she had given them my address as a meeting place. Could they possibly wait and see whether she would turn up.

I wavered. They had been walking since seven o'clock, they pleaded; they had huge rucksacks on their backs, they were almost in tears. I weakened and let them in. I felt smugly conscious of bridging the Generation Gap; the young are not the only ones who can practise universal brotherhood, I thought, as I gave them coffee and biscuits.

They were very sweet and grateful. They admired the children and the house, then asked if I would mind if they left their things in the drawing-room while they nipped out for cigarettes.

It was only an hour later – when worried they might have got lost – I discovered not only had they not left their things behind, they had also stolen £25 from my handbag. The person from Clacton predictably never turned up.

As a result I'm a bit off Youth at the moment – in fact, next time a deb accosts me outside Harrods and asks me for a contribution to National Youth Week, I shall be tempted to ram her slit tin down her throat.

What really irritated me about the whole incident was that I'd been conned rotten. I ought to have realized that in most instances universal brotherhood is only another name for the perpetual scrounging practised by the young. They continually attack my generation for being materialistic, but they'll bleed us white given the opportunity.

Another reason I'm not wild about Youth is they make me feel so guilty – for a start – when they're sourly nibbling away at their horrible health foods. Guilty, in fact, about eating anything, when they're all so thin.

They also make me feel guilty about drinking (none of them seems to touch alcohol) and for talking too much. I was brought up to believe it was polite when you were in a room with someone to attempt to engage them in conversation. But if the younger generation don't feel like it, they don't bother to talk at all. 'Perceiving people non-verbally,' they call it. They seem totally unembarrassed by long silences.

On these counts, I emerge as a portly, sottish, garrulous carnivore – hardly attractive, is it?

Another hang-up I have is not being able to dance the way Youth do. Born and bred on the fox-trot, the current orgiastic shiver defeats me completely. Occasionally I lock myself in my bedroom and gyrate and flail in front of the mirror. I know nothing a consenting adult does in the privacy of her own room can be wrong – but it just looks wrong – not a bit like *Top of the Pops*.

The young also make me feel guilty because I have no desire to go back to Nature and live off the fruits of the earth. I love the country, but it bores me silly after a week or so. I much prefer dreary old London, and I loathe the idea of breaking down the family unit and living in a commune.

I read the most chilling piece about young people in communes recently, under the somewhat ambiguous title 'Getting it Together', telling you how all the adults shared their possessions and the daily tasks and the responsibility for the children; how all decisions were put to the vote and how, to break down sexual inhibitions, members of the commune wrote up on a noticeboard the names of other members with whom they wanted to sleep. Unfortunately it always turned out that everyone wanted Samantha, and no one wanted Janet. But that, said the communards, was life.

Anyway, with three children in the house at the moment, a nanny, a husband, five cats and the bailiffs, I'm practically living in a commune. Even so I have a sneaking feeling I'm not helping everyone to 'recognize their own special excellence', and that the cats ought to be put in charge of hewing wood, my son should tend the mangel-wurzels, and the new baby we've acquired should supervise home-made wine.

I know I should try harder, but somehow I'm not really attracted to the life young people seem to lead today. It's far too spartan, and I'm afraid I have a private bathroom mentality. I loathe the idea of roughing it in sleeping bags and crash pads, and living out of rucksacks (I mean whatever was the point of getting myself sacked from the Brownies). I'm scared stiff of riding on the back of motorbikes and hitch-hiking is absolutely anathema. Whoever wants to ride for miles and miles with someone they haven't been introduced to?

But I suppose it is in the sexual field that the Generation Gap yawns the widest. My generation have a feeling they've missed out on all the permissiveness. In retrospect I rather enjoyed my youth, the only thing I regret about it was that it wasn't sufficiently misspent. I wasn't kissed until I was seventeen and a half.

Last year I employed a girl of eighteen and the first week-end I was staggering downstairs when a naked sailor came out of her bedroom. It was so early in the day that I was too shattered to say anything except 'Good morning.' He wasn't remotely embarrassed. Later, I found him cooking breakfast and he asked me if I'd like one egg or two.

I grow old, I grow old. I shall wear the bottoms of my trousers sawn off and fraying at Bermuda length. All my friends – particularly the men – seem so much better at keeping up with youth. They emerge at parties having jettisoned their unsuccessful pinstripe in place of tasselled handbags and tee-shirts covered with stars. Beards sprout on their chins, and their receding hair is coaxed forward into tendrils to cover their furrowed foreheads.

'We're taking a trip, this weekend,' they say.

'Oh lovely,' say I, 'Brighton?'

And they look at me pitifully and disappear into the next room and start tearing cigarettes apart, and muttering about meaningful life-styles.

The young today want to change the world, my generation only wanted to change their hairstyles. We were the generation of alcohol and abdication, they are the age of pot and participation. Our main pre-occupation was getting a nine-to-five job, they reject such monotony, but beef even more if the unemployment figures are high and there aren't any nine-to-five jobs to reject.

My mother made the classic comment on the situation the other day. She arrived in great excitement – she'd seen a naked girl at the window next door and a car outside with a sticker saying 'Rolling Stones – Sticky Fingers'.

'Who lives there?' she asked.

'Oh lots of hippies,' I said.

'Don't they work' she said, 'don't they even play in a band?'

But what finally convinced me of the Generation Chasm was being in the Mall the other day, when a Royal Coach crammed with Real Live Royalty and all the trappings of coachmen and postillions came by. On one of the horses rode a youth who cannot have been more than seventeen: pink-eared, staring rigidly in front of him. Suddenly, out of the corner of his eye, he saw a pretty girl in the crowd.

'Hullo, darling,' he shouted.

THE STORK CLUB

(AN EXTRACT)

—————————— ♦ ——————————

Maureen Freely

It was, according to the big red clock on the wall, 8.48. I was three minutes late.

Not such a good way to start the school year, perhaps, but not such a bad one either. And anyway, they were late because I hadn't wanted to send them into school crying. Now they were calm. So I had done the right thing, although you wouldn't have known it from the look Fatso gave me.

It was the kind of look you'd expect to get if you ran into a one-night-stand months after the event and said, 'Don't I know you from somewhere?' Except that no, it was even worse than that. It was the kind of look you'd expect if you knocked someone up, ran off to join the Navy, and came back four years later expecting dinner on the table. Reproachful does not even come close to describing it, and because I had never, to my knowledge, set eyes on her before, it both confused me and put me on the defensive, so that at the same time as I was thinking, 'What did I do wrong?' I was also sure I had indeed done something wrong, which sin I had then compounded by forgetting all about it.

Now. I know you are going to say that I was reading things into the situation that were not there. She was simply trying to do her job, I can hear you saying, and this is a school that takes promptness seriously.

But all Fatso had to say was, 'Go into the cloakroom so that

Vampyra can do the check list. These kids are not allowed into my Circle until Vampyra gives me the OK.'

Did she? No. First she had to get even with me for belonging to the same sex as all the dates who had made her feel worthless for being fat. She kept me standing there with my arms flapping while she (a) greeted Jesse with controlled effusion, and then (b) asked him to introduce Maria, and then (c) asked him, with controlled sternness, if he had forgotten some important things, and then, when he couldn't remember, (d) opened the discussion to the floor. Could the other children tell Jesse what they had done before joining Circle? Slowly, painfully, the story emerged: they had had to go into the cloakroom one by one to be processed. 'Otherwise, what would this room look like? It would be covered with coats and shoes and lunchboxes and all sorts of *other* personal effects, wouldn't it? And then we couldn't play, could we? How could we teach our new friend Maria how to play sleeping lions *then*?'

'We couldn't,' said one little horror with a piping voice. 'We would have to scrunch up like underprivileged children.'

'*That's* not a very nice thing to say,' said Fatso. 'Does anybody know why?'

A flock of hands shot up. The last thing I heard as Jesse led me out of the room was, 'So, Donner. Why aren't we supposed to say bad things about kids whose moms and dads don't have as much money as *our* moms and dads have?'

Vampyra was waiting for us in the cloakroom. The moment I saw her I thought: 'Oh my God. I've walked into a Kafka novel'. Because again, I had the strong impression that I had done something wrong and that I was never going to be able to make up for it because she was never going to tell me what it was.

Now I know you all think Vampyra is a really nice woman. Well, not to men she isn't. Despite her standard-issue nursery-school-teacher appearance, there was something about the way she flinched at extraneous noise, and something about the wild fear that would flick in her eyes that made me wonder if she hadn't spent the previous night on a stretcher South of Market being whipped.

In the beginning, she, too, refused to look me in the eyes, although in this case there was more nervousness in her behaviour than disapproval. It was as if she were afraid of being recognized. Every time she turned to Jesse to ask him a question, she would take a big breath first, as if it were a tremendous effort to do her day job properly after whatever it was she had been up to during the night.

I don't know what was more horrifying – her interrogation or the fact that Jesse understood it. When she asked him if I was his primary caretaker this year, he didn't blink an eye. He just said yes, his mother had become the breadwinner. *Breadwinner*. How old was I when I started using that word? Eighteen? Twenty-five? I was also alarmed by how comfortable he was with a term I had always found clinical – namely, sibling. His sibling's name was Maria, he told Vampyra. She was three years old, the same as Ken's sibling. When I asked him, 'Why can't you just say sister?' he said, 'Because it's sexist.'

He then went on to tell me – with Vampyra's prompting – that from now on I would have to be punctual. Tardy children were only allowed in 'at half-hour increments'. He actually knew the word – increment. I could hardly have been less shocked than if he had turned around and said to me, 'By the way, Dad. While you were in the shower last night I joined the Freemasons.' Because that's what this school was beginning to look like to me – a secret society in which I was branded as an outsider because I didn't have the right handshake.

Or the right number of chromosomes.

This first intimation that my son belonged to a world I knew nothing about – it was like getting an electric shock. But I had no time to think what it really meant, and again, this set the pattern for the rest of the week.

Because now, after having ignored me completely, she turned to me and said, 'So. Let's get down to brass tacks. Could you please provide me with two crib sheets plus the two changes of clothing which you have clearly marked in a plastic bag and the two passport-size photographs of the children for their Personal Effects Boxes?'

'Come again?' I said.

She came again.

'Could you please provide me with two crib sheets plus the two changes of clothing which you have clearly marked in a plastic bag plus two passport-size photographs of the children for their Personal Effects Boxes?'

I told her I didn't know I was supposed to bring in any of those things. She stared at me as if I had told her I had a mistress and two illegitimate children in rural Thailand.

'But if you had read the fine print in the contract,' she said, 'You would have known about these requirements.'

'I think my wife must have signed the contract because I never saw it.'

Now she looked at me as if I had just admitted to buying a Guatemalan baby on the black market.

'But that's terrible!' she yelped. 'Because if you are the primary caretaker from now on, there are all sorts of things in there you should have at your fingertips! For one thing, it makes it extremely clear that in order to successfully process your child on the first day of school you must provide all the items I mentioned. I honestly don't know if I can let your children in today, as distressing as that would be for all of us.'

'How about if I go home now and bring back all the things you need by lunchtime?'

She looked at me as if I had said, 'Why don't you throw off all your clothes and do the cancan on the table?'

'I'll have to check with Eva on that,' she said, dubiously, 'i.e., our directress. But first let me check the lunchboxes because we want to make sure we're all clear on the other requirements before we disturb her. As you can imagine, we're up to here today.' She gave me the kind of crazed smile you'd expect from a Baptist spinster who had just accepted a thimble glass of low-alcohol sherry.

Then she opened Jesse's lunchbox.

'ooooooh,' she said. 'ooooooh. You have some fruit rollups in here! That is a no-no! As is white bread, I'm afraid!' Again, her tone of voice was inappropriate. It was as if she were saying, 'Under normal circumstances I would love to, but I'm afraid I can't because you're not wearing a condom.'

And then, when I said, 'It may be white bread, but it's good, it's from a French bakery,' her eyes bulged as if I had assured her not only was I wearing a condom, but it was ribbed.

'This has never happened before!' she exclaimed. 'I don't know what to say. I simply cannot admit them myself if they are carrying inappropriate lunches. I'll have to talk it over with Eva.'

BEDROCK

(AN EXTRACT)

———————— ♦ ————————

Lisa Alther

Descending the cliff, she could see a campfire through the trees, surrounded by several dozen naked women, who were pounding African drums and dripping with sweat. Throwing off her clothes, Barbara sat down. A dried gourd was passed to her, and the circle fell silent. Barbara looked at the rattle. 'I've come from California for the Healing Intensive.'

Everyone opened her eyes to inspect Barbara. 'It was last month,' replied a woman with Buddha-like folds of flesh around her middle and a luminescent blue and yellow parrot on her shoulder. Starshine, the big cheese herself, Ishtar soon learned.

'But the *Amazon Quarterly* said this week.'

'Sorry. A typo.'

'Power to the People!' shrieked the parrot.

'This is Sexuality Week,' said Starshine. 'We're doing a sweat, then a masturbation circle.'

'Whatever,' sighed Barbara. She'd been counting on some healing. Her wounds of maternal abandonment were still running sores.

'Make Love, Not War!' screamed the parrot.

'So what's your preference?' asked Starshine.

Barbara looked at her blankly.

'The rattle. You're holding it. You can describe a fantasy, sing a song, or pass it on. Whatever you want.'

'I guess I'll pass till I get the hang of it.' Barbara handed the rattle to the next woman, Morning Glory as it turned out, who wore a red bandanna headband and a spiral little toe-ring. She asked for the drumming to resume.

During the masturbation circle Barbara fell in love. The other women were self-conscious or matter-of-fact, but Morning Glory really got into it, eyes closing and mouth falling open. Barbara wanted to know her better, so she became Ishtar.

Ishtar came to Vermont on a typo, and stayed out of lust. Sometimes she wondered if the whole thing wasn't one big mistake. When Starshine became aware of the attraction between Ishtar and Morning Glory, she canceled their nights of sleeping together, maintaining that the privatization of their emotions was interrupting group flow. Ishtar tried to accept this, but like a tamed wolf, she'd tasted blood and would have to be shot before she'd give it up. Morning Glory, however, was more docile and kept Ishtar at a distance.

Until one night on forest patrol. Ishtar and Morning Glory went into the barn at the top of the cliff and smoked a joint Ishtar had been hiding from Starshine's inspections in her parka lining. The scent of hay mixed with the acrid marijuana smoke. Ishtar puffed out her cheeks and mimicked Starshine, talking about her superior spiritual incandescence. Morning Glory was both horrified and titillated. Then Ishtar reached over and unbuttoned Morning Glory's flannel shirt. Morning Glory gasped, 'We aren't allowed to do this, Ishtar. Besides, it's my night with Foxglove.'

'Who says we aren't?'

'You know the rules.'

'Fuck the rules. Run away with me, Morning Glory.'

Morning Glory said she would, and Ishtar kissed her little-toe ring and worked up, as the old barn swayed and creaked around them.

But when it came down to packing up and walking away from Mink Creek, Morning Glory backed out.

Meanwhile, Ishtar was having trouble with the Boudicca menu. Because of their refusal to harm any living creature, they were eating a lot of peanut butter and crackers. And because of a chronic money shortage, they were raiding the Dumpster behind Starr's IGA for spoiled produce. This deprivation no doubt explained why Ishtar opened a restaurant after her escape. Which came soon after she read Shirley MacLaine's *Out on a Limb* and realized that by hating men, Boudiccas were storing up some bad karma and might have to return in future lives as rapists.

Starshine instantly announced at a teaching session in the house trailer that she, too, was writing a book, *The Lesbian Book of the Dead*, about how to negotiate one's transition to a higher soul plane, where you could be absorbed into the goddesshead of pure female energy. Ishtar suggested that Starshine title it *Out of Her Tree*. Starshine proceeded to beat her up with karate kicks and punches.

The next day Ishtar was gone. And since then she'd seen Morning Glory only during Boudicca actions outside her café. While the others hassled Ishtar's bewildered customers, Morning Glory in her red bandanna headband would gaze at Ishtar with fear and longing. But it seemed unlikely she'd leave Mink Creek. Ishtar was heartsick. She could rejoin the Boudiccas, but it would be torture to put up with Starshine's guru nonsense.

Ishtar sometimes saw Starshine around town, dressed in a suit, heels, and panty hose, on her way to talk to Alvin Jacobs' Amerikan Gulag class at Camel's Hump Community College about gay rights, or to Conrad Bohring at Mink Valley Savings and Loan about her investments. Sometimes, with a guilty glance around the green, she'd duck into Casa Loretta for a Ridgeburger or a Spam burrito, while her troops in the valley ate peanut butter and crackers. Once when Ishtar ran into Starshine emerging from a taco pizza debauch, she asked, 'Well, well. And how's the Imelda Marcos of Mink Creek?'

Ishtar picked up a spider plant, carried it inside, and hung it near the ceiling amid hundreds of identical plants. En route to the kitchen, Ishtar glanced at the poster on one wall that listed her past lives from 10000 B.C. to the present. So far she'd identified twenty-six. Shirley MacLaine got in touch with hers via acupuncture with golden needles, but Ishtar had had to make do with sterilized straight pins. Some of her prior lives seemed to involve a place very much like Roches Ridge, and people who lived around her now – Father Flanagan, for instance, the Catholic priest in his tight white collar and gold Pro-Life lapel pin, who came to the Karma Café late at night and rambled on about his failings as though in a confessional. And his housekeeper, Theresa, in her funky forties house-dresses with padded shoulders, and her veiled straw pillbox hat decorated with wooden cherries, with whom Ishtar some-times chatted on the green.

At some point she must have been a vegetable, Ishtar reflected, judging from her allegiance to spider plants in this life. Before Calvin Roche left for Texas, she introduced him to reincarnation, explaining how customers who loved sushi had probably been sharks. Pointing to Ishtar's poster, Calvin asked, 'But why stop at 10000 B.C.?'

'You have to draw the line somewhere,' she replied. But it was a good point. Where *did* you draw the line? When she wrote to ask Shirley, she received a mimeographed form wishing her well on her own inner journey toward the light. But if she didn't work through her obsession with past lives this time around, she might get to come back as Shirley MacLaine.

MRS HARTLEY AND THE GROWTH CENTRE

(AN EXTRACT)

◆

Philippa Gregory

The aerobic gardening class was a remarkable success. Stephanie had been hesitant about the concept, arguing wasps and stinging nettles; but when she saw the large hi-fi speakers loaned with unconscious generosity by the university drama centre, and heard the heavy drum beat echoing in the overgrown garden, she was inspired. Alice explained that all aerobic dance was substitute work, performed as an inadequate alternative to hard manual labour. Their bodies were, in fact, crying out for the drudgery of rural toil. Alice grew persuasively anthropological about the alienation of women from their natural work. She explained how women since the dawn of time have heaved things, lifted things, cleared and gardened. Alice urged them to be authentic, to get in touch with their inheritance, with Nature, to get to grips with reality, and offered them – instead of little dances with chopping motions of the hands – the real thing: axes and half a dozen fallen trees to work on.

Ten pupils had arrived for the aerobics class this morning: a pair of identical and indistinguishable twins who introduced themselves shyly as Gary and Timofy, and their friend Jonafon, as well as two new faculty wives, who arrived lugging babies in backpacks and looking harassed.

'Leave them with me!' Alice cried. 'I love babies! And you

must be exhausted. What you need is an hour's aerobo-work and then half an hour's relaxation.'

Two pairs of eyes shadowed black with exhaustion from sleepless nights and loneliness boggled helplessly at Alice.

'Poor darlings!' Alice said to them. 'Babies are a blessing, but such hard work.'

Tears welled up in the eyes of the shorter woman. She staggered slightly as Alice lifted the backpack off her. 'I wanted a pram,' she said sadly. 'But he said that it should be carried. They all say you've got to carry them these days.'

Alice popped the baby out of the backpack like tight-fitting pea from a pod.

'Babies need the feeling of closeness,' said the other woman in a dulled monotone. 'They need to feel close to Mother, all day, all night, every day, every night.'

'Of course,' Alice said, matter-of-fact. 'Of course babies need the feeling of closeness. But *you* need the feeling of distance.'

The second woman gasped, it was as if Alice had sworn in a church.

'They need to hear Mother's heartbeat,' she said, repeating the lesson. 'They need to feel Mother's movement.'

'Oh yes,' Alice agreed readily. 'They'd like that all the time. But they're born now, aren't they? Can't go on listening to your stomach gurgling all their lives. They'll have to get used to it sooner or later. *You* don't get exactly what you want all the time, do you?'

The two young women gazed at Alice with red-rimmed eyes. They looked like long-stay prisoners of the Bastille on the morning of July 14th. They looked like they had *never* got exactly what they wanted – at any time.

The taller one's lip quivered as she fought back tears. 'He won't ever lie in his cot!' she said despairingly. 'He'll only sleep if I walk him. And if I stop walking he wakes up and cries! Up and down on the landing, all night long. I must have walked to London and back half a dozen times. The only time he sleeps is when he hears David's key in the door. As soon as he hears the front door open and David shout, 'I'm home, I've had a bloody awful day, pour me a drink for God's sake,' he falls at once into deep sleep and makes darling little snores and David tells me I'm too tense! He tells me that it's *me* that's keeping him awake. Of course I'm tense!' she said, her voice a squeak of suppressed rage. 'I've not slept for months, I walk farther every night than I've ever walked before in my life, and when I complain David says, 'Really, Suzanne, you wanted the baby, you know.' As if I ever knew what I was getting myself into!'

Alice clucked comfortingly. 'Little horror,' she said with a loving smile. 'Tuck him in bed beside you, lovey, and drink a stiff gin before you feed him. It'll settle him down in no time.'

The shorter woman gulped. 'If you knew ...' she started, her sobs drowning out her words. Alice, with the baby gurgling wetly over one shoulder, reached out her spare arm and gathered the miserable mother to her capacious breast.

'I know,' she said sweetly. 'Let the tears come, my darling. Cry it out.'

'He wakes at two in the morning – on the dot!' the woman shrieked into Alice's shoulder. 'And all Stephen does is kick me awake and say "Baby's crying"!'

Alice nodded and swayed on her feet, rocking mother and child at once.

'He hates my milk!' she sobbed. 'I know he does! He makes miserable faces when I try to feed him, and his nappies are filled with brown Camembert! And when I take him down to the clinic all the babies there are on the dreadful artificial milk which stresses their kidneys and makes them sugar addicts. But *they* are all cooing and getting fat, and their mothers stick a bottle in their mouths and go off and have coffee together. And when he's weighed the health visitor just looks at me and says – ' she gasped. 'She says ... s-s-supplementary bottle! It makes me feel so inferior!' She gulped herself to a standstill.

Alice murmured understandingly.

'I know they think I'm not feeding him enough!' she wailed. 'But he looks at me as if he thinks the whole idea is disgusting. And *I* think it's disgusting. I have to mess about with these ghastly bras and these little bits of tissue! And Stephen keeps going on and on about how I should be loving the experience of getting up every half hour! And Stephen's read *all* the books and they all go on and on about African babies being carried all the time, and being breast-fed until they are four, and never getting depressed when they are teenagers because they bonded right. African babies don't get separation anxiety! African babies wean themselves! And when I say I want a drink or a cigarette, or to go out for the evening, he says to me: "African babies don't get left with a babysitter!"'

'Silver Cross prams!' cried the other mother. 'They sit in their prams, those fat, bottle-fed, happy little things, and smile at me while I lug him about on my back. I was heaving him around like a sack of coal before I even had the stitches out!'

Alice hummed softly and let Mother and baby snivel into each side of her neck.

'Baby-bouncers!' said the first mother, it was like a prayer for release. 'I want a baby-bouncer so I can stick him in it and *leave* him. Just for five minutes!'

'Play-pen!' said the other, like an invocation. 'Just *think* of being allowed a play-pen!'

Alice patted the shorter mother's shoulder with one hand and jiggled the baby on the other arm. She smiled steadily at the other young mother who was nodding wearily and lowering her baby-pack to the ground like Pilgrim getting rid of the fruits of his sins. As soon as the pack touched ground the baby opened his mouth and let out a great bellow of discontent. Both mothers flinched as if they had been struck.

'Now you run along,' Alice said clearly above the noise. The second baby had started up now. The two mothers quivered where they stood like windlashed weak-stemmed tulips. 'I'll look after these two. The crèche is ten pounds an hour and we give them massage and flower extracts. You'll see. They'll be new babies when you collect them.'

She took a squalling infant on each hip, and showed the bedraggled mothers out to the orchard. Stephanie watched them approach with huge black eyes in her white face, jogging lightly from one bony foot to another.

Alice waited while they turned up the music and did some warm-up exercises, the usual mimes of stamping down a new-laid lawn, hoeing a flower-bed, and pushing a lawn-mower; and then Stephanie directed them to the garden tools and they put their energy into the real thing.

Alice swayed inside, each baby clinging like a small greedy parasite on a new host.

'Now,' she said, looking from one to another. 'What do you two need?'

She laid them gently on their backs on the kitchen table. At the unknown sensation of being left in a bit of peace both babies contracted their faces and squalled miserably. Alice stepped back a pace and looked at them.

'Floral extracts,' she said to herself, and turned towards the larder.

She came back with a magnum-sized wine bottle stoppered with thick cork. She struggled to open it while the wails from the babies grew louder and more pained. She poured the foaming liquid into a wine glass and took a sip herself. Then carefully, and with patience, she spooned the sparkling clear liquid into each of the hot, wide, noisy mouths.

Both babies were as suddenly silenced as if someone had succumbed to temptation and held a pillow over their heads. The little faces scrunched up while they assessed this new taste which was not dreary old milk nor dull old water, but something dramatically different. Slowly, little toothless beams appeared on their cross faces. Alice spooned in some more, and supported Baby no. 1 as he coughed.

Alice went to the big kitchen cupboard where all sorts of household utensils had been stored, and heaved an old wash-board and a wringer out of the way. At the back was a big carriage-built perambulator, massive on bouncy leather straps; more like a landau than a pram. Alice heaved it out, wiped it down, threw in a couple of blankets and sat a baby at each end.

They smiled. They pointed at each other and gurgled. They had seen nothing but their mothers' backs for months, and the change of scenery was welcome. They lay back and watched the sunlight on the kitchen wall. Then they sneezed and giggled at the noise. They had heard nothing but their own mournful bellowing for weeks and their mothers' strained voices. Alice pulled up a chair beside the pram and poured herself another glass from the brown bottle, and gave each baby a sip more.

A party mood was rapidly developing, as the babies goggled around with blue unfocused eyes and Alice joggled the pram with her bare feet. She gave one a tea strainer to look at, and the other a wooden spoon to chew. Both babies accepted these mundane gifts with idiotic enthusiasm. Always before they had been forced to work on brightly coloured educational toys designed to inspire their curiosity, stimulate small-muscle work and develop dexterity. It had really pissed them off. Now they had a chance to get hold of a simple object and hammer the hell out of it on the side of the pram.

It was obviously a big relief. Alice smiled fondly at them both.

Baby no. 2 burped richly and they both creased up as at a dinner-table *bon mot*. Alice giggled too and gave them another spoonful each.

Baby no. 1 started chewing on the handle of the wooden spoon. He drooled blissfully sucking in the impregnated taste of long-ago meals and well-washed wood. Everything at home tasted the same: of sterilizing fluid. This was just great. He cooed.

THE CONTRIBUTORS

◆

ALTHER, Lisa: American author of a series of feminist novels beginning with *Kinflicks* in 1972.

ARNOLD, Sue: Columnist for *The Observer* and various magazines.

AYRES, Pam: Comic poet who regards her playful puns and ghastly rhymes as being more music hall than literature.

BOMBECK, Erma: American agony aunt, humorist, broadcaster and author of numerous books of comic advice about family life.

BYRNE, Dorothy: Poet.

COOPER, Jilly: Comic writer, journalist and blockbuster novelist.

COPE, Wendy: Poet and parodist notable for very contemporary, stylish verse about modern relationships and men.

CROMPTON, Richmal: Best-known for her hugely popular *William* stories. Created 38 collections from 1922 to 1970.

DE MONTAGNA, Sybylla: Humorous writer, contributor to the recently launched female humour magazine *Bitch*.

DILLER, Phyllis: American comedienne and writer best known for television appearances in the 1950s and 60s.

EPHRON, Nora: American journalist, novelist and screenwriter. Her work includes *Heartburn* and *When Harry Met Sally*.

FIELDING, Helen: Journalist, regular contributor to *The Sunday Times*.

FREELY, Maureen: American novelist and journalist living in Britain. Columnist for the *Independent on Sunday*.

FRENCH, Dawn and Jennifer SAUNDERS: Comic duo who emerged from stand-up cabaret and the Comic Strip company, to create a uniquely female form of alternative comedy.

GIBBONS, Stella: Comic novelist documenting English life between the wars. Her masterpiece is *Cold Comfort Farm*.

GRAHAM, Laurie: Author of several humorous but practical guides to modern life – on marriage, children and etiquette.

GREER, Germaine: Famous for her feminist polemics such as *The Female Eunuch* in 1972 and her study of the menopause, *The Change*, 1991.

GREGORY, Philippa: Author of historical romances, has also written children's books and comic fiction.

GRENFELL, Joyce: Consummately English comedienne, best-known for the characters created through her monologues.

HARRISON, Sarah: Best-known for her romantic historical novels – the first, *Flower of the Fields*, was a saga set during the First World War. She has also written comic novels.

HEIMEL, Cynthia: American journalist and humorist, columnist for the New York *Village Voice* and author of several humorous books including *Sex Tips for Girls*.

KAHN, Alice: American columnist and humorist.

KING, Florence: American novelist and humorist whose best-known work includes *Confessions of a Southern Lady*.

LEBOWITZ, Fran: World-weary New York humorist and journalist.

LEDERER, Helen: Stand-up comic specialising in the nervous, neurotic new woman.

LIMB, Sue: Novelist, playwright and humorist who created the Wordsworth parody, *The Wordsmiths of Gorsemere*, for BBC Radio 4 as well as her *Guardian* alter ego Dulcie Domum.

LIPMAN, Maureen: Actress, comedienne and writer.

LOCHHEAD, Liz: Scottish poet and playwright.

McFADDEN, Cyra: Author and journalist whose satirical portrayal of hip California, *The Serial*, originally appeared in the *San Francisco Chronicle*.

MARK, Jan: Children's author who has written for all ages but specialises in books for teenagers.

MITFORD, Nancy: Author of a series of strongly autobiographical comic novels dealing with upper-class English society between the wars.

MURRAY, Jenni: Writer and broadcaster, presenter of Radio 4's *Woman's Hour*.

NICHOLLS, Grace: Poet and novelist living in Britain, originally from Guyana.

PARKER, Dorothy: New York writer and critic, mistress of the *bon mot* and a member of the charmed Algonquin Round Table in the 1930s.

PITT-KETHLEY, Fiona: Humorous poet renowned for being outspoken and daring about sex, men and romance.

PURVES, Libby: Broadcaster and journalist, presenter of Radio 4's *Midweek* and regular columnist for *The Times*.

SPARK, Muriel: Novelist specialising in sardonic, stylish and witty black comedies.

STEINEM, Gloria: American feminist, writer, journalist and creator of *Ms Magazine*.

THOMAS ELLIS, Alice: Author of a number of darkly comic novels and very funny journalism.

TOWNSEND, Sue: Novelist, playwright and creator of the much-loved teenager Adrian Mole.

TRUSS, Lynne: Journalist, regular columnist for *The Times*.

TWEEDIE, Jill: Journalist, broadcaster and novelist whose *Letters from a Faint-hearted Feminist* originally appeared in *The Guardian*.

WHITEHORN, Katharine: Doyenne of female journalism, who has a celebrated, regular column in *The Observer*.

WOOD, Victoria: Comic actress, playwright, performer, songwriter whose television shows have made her one of Britain's best-loved talents.

ACKNOWLEDGEMENTS

◆

We are grateful to the following (listed alphabetically by author) for permission to reproduce copyright material:

Penguin Books Ltd for the extract from *Bedrock* by Lisa Alther ©Lisa Alther Inc 1990. The *Observer* Newspaper for 'Bosom Buddies and Baddies' by Sue Arnold ©The *Observer*. Pam Ayres for 'Aerobics' from *Pam Ayres: The Works*, published by BBC Books, ©Pam Ayres 1992. Desmond Elliott on behalf of Jilly Cooper for 'Against Youth' from *Jolly Super* by Jilly Cooper. Faber & Faber Ltd for 'My Lover' by Wendy Cope, from *Making Cocoa for Kingsley Amis*, ©Wendy Cope. Macmillan & Co Ltd for 'The Sweet Little Girl in White' from *Still William* by Richmal Crompton. The Suchin Company on behalf of Phyllis Diller for 'Household Hints' from *Titters* by Phyllis Diller. Duckworth UK Ltd for 'The Right Approach' from *More Home Live* by Alice Thomas Ellis. Helen Fielding for 'A Girl's Inner Security', which originally appeared in *The Sunday Times* style section. Maureen Freely for the extract from *The Stork Club* first published by Bloomsbury, ©Maureen Freely 1992. The Peters, Fraser & Dunlop Group Ltd for 'Woman's World' from *A Feast of French and Saunders* by Dawn French & Jennifer Saunders. Extract from *Cold Comfort Farm* by Stella Gibbons by permission of Curtis Brown Ltd on behalf of the author's estate. Random House UK Ltd for the extract from *The Parents' Survival Guide* by Laurie Graham. Aitken & Stone Ltd on behalf of Germaine Greer for 'Going Without'. Rogers, Coleridge & White Ltd on behalf of Philippa Gregory for the extract from *Mrs Hartley and the Growth Centre*, ©Philippa Gregory. Macmillan & Co Ltd for 'In Committee' from *Stately as a Galleon & Other Songs and Sketches* by Joyce Grenfell. Little Brown & Co (UK) Limited for the extract from *Hot Breath* by Sarah Harrison. Fourth Estate Ltd for 'How to Get a Man' from *If You Can't Live Without Me, Why Aren't You Dead?* by Cynthia Heimel. William Morris Agency (UK) Ltd on behalf of Florence King for 'Roll me Over, Lay me Down' ©Florence King 1974, first published in *Playgirl* in the USA. Extract from *Amassed Hysteria* by Helen Lederer reprinted by permission of the Richard Stone Partnership. Fourth Estate Ltd for the extract from *Dulcie Domum's Bad Housekeeping* by Sue Limb. Robson Books Ltd for 'A Joking Aside' from *How Was It for You* by Maureen Lipman. A. P. Watt Ltd on behalf of Liz Lochhead for 'Vymura: the Shade Card Poem' by Liz Lochhead. Abner Stein on behalf of Cyra McFadden for 'Hip Wedding on Mount Tam' and 'A Visit to the Vets' from *The Serial* by Cyra McFadden. Random House UK Ltd for 'Drug-Crazed Thugs Wrecked my Lounge' from *Enough is Too Much Already* by Jan Mark. Extract from *Love in a Cold Climate* by Nancy Mitford reprinted by permission of the Peters, Fraser & Dunlop Group Ltd. *Too Tired to Want to Go Home* by Jenni Murray printed with the permission of the *Woman's Hour* team, who have been much maligned. Virago for 'The Fat Black Woman Goes Shopping' from *The Fat Black Woman's Poems* by Grace Nicholls. Duckworth & Co Ltd for 'Re-enter Margot Asquith' from *The Collected Dorothy Parker* by Dorothy Parker. Random House UK Ltd for 'Penis Envy' from *Sky Ray Lolly* by Fiona Pitt-Kethley. Libby Purves for 'Madam and the Mini-Bar' which originally appeared in *Punch*, ©Libby Purves 1987. Macmillian & Co Ltd for the extract from *The Prime of Miss Jean Brodie* by Muriel Spark. Levine, Thall & Plotkin for 'If Men Could Menstruate' from *Outrageous Acts and Everyday Rebellions* by Gloria Steinem, published by Holt, Rinehart & Winston ©1983 by Gloria Steinem. First published in *Ms* Magazine, October 1978. Extract from *The Secret Diary of Adrian Mole Aged 13¾* by Sue Townsend reprinted by permission of Methuen, London. David Higham Associates on behalf of Lynne Truss for 'Too Late, Too Late' by Lynne Truss. Jill Tweedie and Pan Books Ltd for an extract from *Letters from a Faint-Hearted Feminist* by Jill Tweedie. Katharine Whitehorn for 'Sluts', ©Katharine Whitehorn. 'Kitty' from *Up to You Porky* by Victoria Wood, reprinted by permission of Methuen, London.

The compiler and publishers have made every effort to trace copyright holders of material reproduced in this anthology. If, however, they have inadvertently made any error they would be grateful for notification.